T0102359

Developing Your Supernatural Awareness

Connecting with an Interactive Universe

Also by this Author
*Perceptual Hypnosis: A Spiritual Journey Toward
Expanding Awareness*
978-0764353109

Developing
Your Supernatural
Awareness

Connecting with an Interactive Universe

Fredrick Woodard

6TH
BOOKS

Winchester, UK
Washington, USA

JOHN HUNT PUBLISHING

First published by Sixth Books, 2024
Sixth Books is an imprint of John Hunt Publishing Ltd., No. 3 East St., Alresford,
Hampshire SO24 9EE, UK
office@jhpbooks.com
www.johnhuntpublishing.com
www.6th-books.com

For distributor details and how to order please visit the 'Ordering' section on our website.

Text copyright: Fredrick Woodard 2023

ISBN: 978 1 80341 478 2
978 1 80341 479 9 (ebook)
Library of Congress Control Number: 2022952061

All rights reserved. Except for brief quotations in critical articles or reviews, no part of this
book may be reproduced in any manner without prior written permission from the publishers.

The rights of Fredrick Woodard as author have been asserted in accordance with the Copyright,
Designs and Patents Act 1988.

A CIP catalogue record for this book is available from the British Library.

Design: Matthew Greenfield

UK: Printed and bound by CPI Group (UK) Ltd, Croydon, CR0 4YY
Printed in North America by CPI GPS partners

We operate a distinctive and ethical publishing philosophy in
all areas of our business, from our global network of authors to
production and worldwide distribution.

Contents

Dedication

This book is dedicated to those individuals who have shared and continue to share their supernatural experiences and knowledge with me. They have given me unusual gifts that I will always cherish.

Acknowledgments

Thank you to the following: Dr. Errol Leifer and Dr. Shelley Stokes at the California School of Professional Psychology in Fresno, California, where I obtained my doctorate, for allowing me to work freely on new ideas I had formulated about hypnosis, spirituality, and perception. Drs. Carol and Douglas Ammons of Ammons Scientific for working with me on numerous journal articles that are fundamental to my writing and research that are now with Sage Publications. Gregor Bernard for illustrating these experiences. Kelly Griffin for contributing her photograph. Amy Rost for her editorial suggestions and guidance. Gavin L. Davies of 6th Books and his marketing and editorial staff (including Elizabeth Radley, Frank Smecker, Krystina Kellingley, Mary Flatt, Nick Welch, Steve Wagstaff) for their assistance in publishing this book.

I especially want to thank a few individuals who have had a great impact on my life's journey and soul's evolution: My maternal grandfather, William Abel, for encouraging me to never give up! Dr. Anne Cohen Richards for her support in encouraging me to put my ideas into manuscripts for journal articles and books. Dr. Pierre Dionne, Dr. Robert Kaladish, Dr. Katerina Tolstikova, and Dr. David Underwood for their support and encouragement. My many cousins, Abel, Kirk, Lefebvre, Riccardo, and Woodard families, for their emotional support through the years, especially Joyce Woodard, Danni Hall Woodard, Lori Woodard Richey. Charles and Tim Shay, my distant cousins and descendants of Chief Madockawando, for sharing their Native American experiences with me.

Introduction

When you have a supernatural experience, you may accept or reject it. You may want to believe it happened but just can't let yourself think that thought. You might want to reject it, but something is telling you there is more to it. If you are open to such an experience, or believe that there is more to it, the next step is to explore what has happened.

I once watched a twenty-eight-year-old married woman wrestle with a childhood supernatural experience as she sat in my office. As she talked, she glanced away from me periodically. She said she had never told a psychologist or anyone this story, which happened when she was six years old.

Her mother had remarried, and she and her stepfather "had such a great relationship." Then one day she woke up at 2 a.m. to see him standing by her bed. He said, "I need you to be strong. I need you to take care of your mother and your sister. I will not be returning home."

"I thought that was odd because he was standing in front of me," the woman told me.

"I said, 'But you're here. What do you mean you're not coming home?'"

He said to her, "You'll understand."

"I went and I woke my mother up because I thought I had been having a nightmare," the woman continued. "And about twenty minutes after I had woken her up, the hospital called, wanting her to come and identify his body. He had been in a car accident and had been killed."

Her mother seemed to think the girl's vision of her stepfather was just her imagination or perhaps a dream. It seemed like her mother didn't think what she was telling her was real. Her mother's response left her feeling "numb" and wanting "to just do nothing more than want to go outside and play" because she didn't know what else to do. She couldn't have really seen a ghost, could she?

This woman wasn't the first person to come into my office with a ghost story. And her mother wasn't the first person to wonder what her loved one's alleged ghost encounter meant— or even if it was real. Many people have sought me out to tell me stories like this or their stories of encountering aliens, angels, and demons. Some people have foreseen a person's death. Others have communicated with animals in unusual ways. Others have experienced synchronicities that were just so uncanny that they couldn't possibly just be chalked up to coincidence.

People come to me with their stories because they've heard that I won't just write off their experiences as signs of depression, anxiety, or another mental health condition. I'm known as the psychologist who has an open mind toward such experiences. Not only that, but I can also help people make sense of what they experienced.

My interest in the supernatural isn't just academic or clinical. I've had many unusual experiences in my journey to understand consciousness. I've had strange synchronistic events in which I've encountered animals, found coins, and experienced happenings just after I'd seen or thought about such things in my mind. The events seemed to be mere coincidences when looked at logically. However, the chances that my thoughts and the same real-world details would occur together seemed out of the ordinary. These coincidences were unimportant to anyone else, but they held personal meaning for me as an individual.

An example of one such incident occurred while I was doing genealogy research at the New Hampshire State Library in Concord. I had traced my ancestors back from the present to Captain Amos Woodard in Pittsford, Vermont. I had also traced the lineage of the man I thought to be his father, Joshua

Woodard, all the way back to Boston, in the 1600s. But I just could not find any documents to verify their connection as father and son.

As I was looking through birth records and other records, I heard two elderly men talking at a whisper in the corner of the room. I could hardly make out what they were saying. Suddenly, in my head, I heard one of their voices say very loudly, "Check the land deeds." His voice then returned to near-inaudible mumbling.

I requested the land deeds for Pittsford, Vermont, for the appropriate time period from the Latter-day Saints library in Nashua, New Hampshire. Among them I found a land deed stating that Captain Amos Woodard was buying property from his "honored mother Mary Woodard," on 17, February 1792. I knew from my previous research that Joshua's wife was named Mary. There was my proof that Joshua and Amos were father and son. (It should be noted that it is rare to find land deeds to include any statements about the relationship of the parties involved.)

How did those specific words, "Check the land deeds," get magnified in my mind? And how did the words and this information come together in such a meaningful way? Was my unconscious mind tapping into past history? Was a spirit or ancestor communicating with me? Or was something else at work? I never have truly come to understand how this odd experience led me to the information I was seeking. However, I did conclude that studying such experiences would help me understand them. Studying them would also be a way of distinguishing valid, authentic supernatural experiences from invalid or inauthentic ones (experiences that might seem supernatural because we don't immediately see the logical, real-world connections between them), and from psychotic or wishful-thinking experiences, where we want something to be authentic that is not.

I sought out people and events that could help me gain a greater understanding of supernatural experiences. I attended psychic-development workshops and Wiccan ceremonies. I visited mediums. I participated in Native American ceremonies at Tule River Reservation at Porterville, California, and Indian Island in Maine, where my cousin Tim Shay led spiritual ceremonies. I remember on one of those evenings when Tim was leading a ceremony, I wondered if my great-grandfather from the late 1690s, Chief Madockawando, a grand sachem of the Abenaki nation, was looking down on us. I wondered if he could see Tim and me, his two great-grandchildren, after so many years, coming together in a spiritual way and that we both, in our own ways, were helping others as he had done.

I've met a number of significant people in my explorations of the supernatural. As a child, I had the mentorship of my maternal grandfather and my parish priest, both of whom always encouraged me to seek greater understanding by choosing direct experience over common information and assumptions about things. My grandfather also taught me the mind can do incredible things, and he was always pointing out new ways of seeing things. Many clients, friends, girlfriends, relatives, students, and teachers shared with me experiences that were transformative for them and pointed toward something more going on in our world than we have been taught to commonly perceive. I met Walter Friesendorf, a volunteer with the Mutual UFO Network (MUFON) and lifetime seeker of the metaphysical; he used to send me referrals for people who had been abducted by aliens and had other supernatural experiences. He and I would often have in-depth supernatural discussions as we hiked together in the woods with my German shepherds, Shadow and Kiara.

I wondered what all the various unusual experiences I investigated had in common. I innately knew they meant something important, but what? Each of them was definitely an opportunity for the person experiencing them to perceive things in new ways. For example, someone might feel their way through an experience, intuit information from unknown sources, or feel the energy of another person or an event in their body like chills. Someone might hear words or voices in their mind but not necessarily in their outer world. Someone could see a phenomenon as taking them away from their world or see it as part of their world. Perhaps this expansion of perceptual awareness is what caught my attention. Perceptual awareness is any way we take in information from our universe. Supernatural awareness is specifically the ways we take in accurate information from the universe while not being quite sure how we obtained this knowledge. Supernatural experiences, often presented with many different labels, tend to take us beyond the limitations in our body, mind, emotions, and spirit, causing us to look at our personal world or the universe in brand new ways.

Professionally I sought out education in psychology and hypnosis as further ways to understand and study consciousness. I have three master's degrees in psychology and a PhD in clinical psychology. I am a certified hypnotherapist and a licensed clinical psychologist. I've published a number of peer-reviewed journal articles on hypnosis, psychotherapy, and paranormal experiences.

Now, with this book, I explore what different supernatural experiences have in common and how they can transform us. Since 2002, I've interviewed more than 100 individuals about their supernatural experiences, and countless others have informally shared theirs with me. This firsthand research includes cases of people finding missing objects by extraordinary means; having premonitions of future events; encountering supernatural beings, such as angels and the spirits of dead loved ones; communicating in unusual ways with animals; causing electronic devices to malfunction through an energy exchange; and seeing unusual objects.

As I'll explain in Chapter 1, my training as a clinical and phenomenological psychologist has helped me develop a method for interviewing individuals about their supernatural experiences in a thorough and scientific manner that doesn't alter the meanings they place on these events in their lives. Through this phenomenological process, I have identified what certain types of supernatural experiences have in common, what many supernatural experiences in general have in common, and what many individuals commonly experience as they encounter the supernatural and then make sense of what occurred. It's also allowed me to examine individuals' subjective experiences and share how they processed those experiences, found meaning in them, and changed as a result.

I have always been humbled by the unlimited possibilities in our personal world and in the universe. These possibilities are available to each of us, and they are so numerous that they far outweigh any attempts by others to control our minds or manipulate facts to support false beliefs for their own self-gain. We are connected to the earth and to the air we breathe. Our exhalations are needed by the plants to survive. The circle of life allows us to eat and live in a chain of interconnectedness with other forms of life. Our ancestors and family members created all sorts of roots and associations for us. Our culture and prior cultures created our present moment. Our friends and coworkers, our community and our world, spin even more relationships and affiliations. There are so many possible sources from which our supernatural experiences can sprout and grow. Perhaps even past lives, other universes, and other dimensions are affecting us in ways we haven't even begun to understand. Is each of us the same essence of spirit in different bodies in different lives? Is a spiritual battle being fought between good and evil beings or forces on the earth? Understanding the full picture of such complex ideas would take much more than the short one hundred years of one lifetime.

So let us begin.

Chapter 1

Making a Connection

As both a clinical psychologist and paranormal researcher, I'm uniquely qualified to help people who experience things like psychic phenomena and encounters with aliens, ghosts, demons, or angels. I not only validate their experiences (something not many psychologists are willing to do), but also support these individuals as they find meaning in what happened.

Understanding and finding meaning in a supernatural experience is essential. To do so, the experiencer has to be able to make a meaningful connection between the event and their life. I began studying supernatural experiences to help others understand and enhance the supernatural awareness that is part of those experiences, so they can further validate and enhance the unfolding of that supernatural awareness in their everyday life. Supernatural awareness is the unexplained ways we pick up correct information from the world around us, including its unseen or extraordinary aspects. Our supernatural awareness allows us to take in information in ways we may not fully understand.

You may have had a supernatural experience yourself, or maybe you know someone who has. Or perhaps you simply believe such experiences are possible, and you want to explore the unknown by directly experiencing it. Whatever your experience with the supernatural has been so far, this book can be useful to you.

You'll meet more than fifty individuals who've had supernatural experiences, ranging from someone whose energy affected electronic devices to someone who communicated with dolphins at a distance to someone who found a missing insurance document after a visit from her dead father. You'll hear people share stories of aliens, anomalies, psychic phenomena, ghosts, demons, and more. You'll also sit beside me, the psychologist, and observe how they talk about what happened. Within their words is a wealth of information, revealing how people come to understand their experiences and find meaning in them. By seeing firsthand how others have done that, you'll be prepared to do it for yourself.

When I interviewed people, I did not restrict what they chose to call their supernatural experiences. I'd previously explored many different situations that were given various labels, such as *paranormal, spiritual, mystical,* or *metaphysical.* Even some religious experiences seem to wander into the area of the unexplained. When I explored the original definitions of these various terms in the *Oxford English Dictionary,* and the way the average person was using these terms, it seemed that *metaphysical* and *paranormal* implied something beyond the physical, logical, and natural as it is known and taught to us. *Mystical* and *spiritual* added a connection to something beyond religion as we understand it. But as I developed my original research and methodology, I came to label all these experiences for this project as *supernatural.* That term seemed to capture the wide range of unusual experiences everyday people presented to me for examination.

I define *supernatural* as the many evolving parts of our perceiving of awareness (body, mind, emotions, and spirit) that go beyond our commonly-held understandings and the physical limitations of our world. Supernatural experiences challenge what everyday life experiences have mentally programmed us to believe. The question is, are these supernatural experiences really so unusual? In other words, do we sometimes simply not perceive what is actually going on around us? Perhaps by developing our supernatural awareness, we are really just reawakening something that was put to sleep a long time ago.

As a psychologist, I haven't been satisfied with general psychological explanations of hypnosis and altered states, as those explanations have appeared in the psychological literature. They do not completely reflect my own personal and clinical experience. My desire to better understand supernatural experiences led me first to study hypnosis, then to learn meditation, and then to train in psychology and science. Ultimately, I developed my own research methodology after studying for my PhD in clinical psychology.[1] That methodology is a way of scientifically investigating consciousness through direct experiences, as lived and described by everyday people. I was seeking a scientific way of enhancing and exploring people's supernatural experiences, without altering or distorting those experiences in any way. That search may sound simple, but it often has been a very difficult and tedious process.

I began by placing advertisements in several local newspapers, on my website, and on several paranormal websites, seeking individuals who had had unusual, spiritual, or paranormal experiences. People would call my office or send e-mails if they were interested in participating in my research. I would make arrangements to interview them on the telephone, through e-mail or Internet chat, or in person. I wanted to hear their firsthand accounts. I wanted to discover and understand what all of their supernatural experiences had in common. My goal was to find a way to enhance people's openness to supernatural awareness and help those who wish to have a genuine supernatural experience do just that.

The interviews I conducted were in depth. People would tell me their stories, and then I would ask questions that invited them to expand on their meanings and descriptions. I continued to do so until their words revealed no new details or meanings. When I asked questions or said things back to them, I was careful to do so in a way that didn't alter the meaning their words expressed. For example, if someone said they felt "energized" after their supernatural experience, I would say, "Can you say more about that?" That question invited them to expand on what they meant by "energized," without me trying to guess or put words in their mouth.

Here's an example of this process of questioning:

Me: You said, "I could just feel my aunt and uncle." Can you say more about that?

Participant: You mean, like, feeling about the presence in the apartment like we weren't alone?

Me: You said, "I could just feel my aunt and uncle." Can you say more about that?

Participant: The presence was like when you walk into a room. When I walk in and I see you, I know that it's you. I had that same feeling when I walked in. I couldn't see them, but it was the same feeling. I walked in, and I just knew who it was. I could just feel that presence there.

Often it took several sessions for someone to unwrap and express the meanings they placed on their words. For example, "I felt good" can have several different meanings. For one person, feeling good meant "I felt safe and warm." For another, feeling good was "a sense of being happy and carefree."

This interview method respected the individuals' inner events while helping both them and me to draw out the meaning of their experiences. It allowed me to understand each person's experience from their individual perspective. Using this methodology meant I had to put my past experiences and knowledge aside and assume I knew nothing about supernatural experiences.

After each interview, I reviewed it and identified any unsaid details and characteristics, staying with the individual's point of view. This methodology, often referred to as *phenomenological*, is very laborious and lengthy and, as a result, is avoided by many professionals.

Finally, after fifteen years and more than a hundred firsthand interviews, I concluded that each individual's story was a mini version of an awakening to their own supernatural awareness. Now, in this book, I'm presenting this knowledge as a way of helping you develop your own supernatural awareness.

Parts I and II present cases that demonstrate essential types of supernatural experiences, including those that happen out of the blue, those in which a first thought that comes to someone's mind then is corroborated by something in their external experience, those in which an individual's sense of time and space is altered, those in which individuals perceived information through unusual thoughts and feelings, and those in which individuals interacted with external supernatural influences, such as angels, demons, and other creatures. There are also examples of supernatural experiences in which people perceived unfamiliar objects and beings and communicated with spirits of the dead.

Along the way, I address many cutting-edge and controversial aspects of supernatural experiences. Being able to communicate with animals psychically from a distance is one example of a cutting-edge aspect. The notion that demonic energies can affect our physical bodies is an example of a controversial aspect.

In presenting each case, I've stayed as close as possible to the wording the individuals used to describe their supernatural experience during their interview. I've intentionally included a lot of what they said, so you can hear for yourself how they described their experience, how they expanded on their descriptions as the interviews progressed, and how meaning gradually emerged as they shared their stories. Although I've included as much detail about each person as possible, I've omitted or changed people's names to pseudonyms and changed other identifying details to protect their identities. Some people provided more details of their backgrounds than others. Some interviews were formal, and some stories were told in informal settings.

In Part III, I discuss the need for integrity and ethics when dealing with some supernatural beings, the key things supernatural experiences and those who have them have in common, and things to keep in mind when you are dealing with people who are skeptical of supernatural experiences and awareness.

At the end of each chapter, I provide reflections and exercises to help you nurture your own growing supernatural awareness. If you have already had a supernatural experience, this work will help you process and further understand it and its meaning for you. Looking back on your initial supernatural experience, you may realize you have significantly changed for the better because of what happened and what you learned from it. Like most transformative experiences, supernatural experiences can change you without you even realizing it. Looking at the meaning behind your supernatural experiences can enhance your ability to deal with fundamental issues in your life.

When you develop your supernatural awareness, you have access to information from the universe that may help you achieve your personal goals more easily, increase your happiness by improving your relationships and interactions with others, and steer you away from dangers you otherwise would have been oblivious to. It can also help increase your self-awareness, which in turn can allow you to counteract restricting influences in your life. In addition, understanding the different types of supernatural experiences may help you have new or further ones.

You were born with the potential to experience the supernatural. If you already have, reading how others made sense of their experiences, and benefited from them, will help you feel less alone. If you haven't had supernatural experiences yet but want to, this book can prime your supernatural awareness for such experiences.

When you're entering uncharted territory, the battle for truth is far from simple. The opponents often have distorted perspectives. For example, someone may perceive a deceased grandmother or aunt reaching out from "the other side" to attempt to stop a negative event from happening in their lives. A medical professional might label this experience a hallucination worthy of medication. A religious leader to call it evil. Both perspectives are likely based on false assumptions. You must learn to distinguish reality-based occurrences that can be validated by external circumstances from inaccurate distortions that can't be validated. Sometimes genuine supernatural experiences cannot be validated; however, they may make sense in other ways.

A woman with intense fear being soothed and calmed by her dead grandfather appearing in her bedroom and telling her, "You are going to be okay," is an experience that defies scientific explanation. Rather than debate whether this grandfather's presence is real or imagined, I think we should look at the results of this experience and, if the results were positive, validate the meaning of this experience for this person. Just because I may have never seen a red bird before does not mean red birds do not exist. It only means I have not experienced such a bird in my life. We must untangle these subjective moments accurately. In the case of the woman who saw her dead grandfather, the positive, meaningful outcome confirms that hers was an authentic supernatural experience, rather than a hallucination.

I caution you against projecting your wishes onto neutral situations. This can happen when you've had a genuine supernatural experience and want to have more as soon as possible. But also do not let the opinions of others who've had no experiences in this realm interfere with the integrity of your own subjective truth. Regarding validating experiences and dealing with skeptics, I have concluded that subjective truth is self-evident to an individual. Many supernatural experiences do not need to be replicated because they helped someone gain awareness and work through a particular situation efficiently. However, as you learn that many new things are possible, you may well begin having more diverse supernatural experiences. And these transformative experiences can jumpstart or expand your supernatural awareness.

Part I

Changes in Your Perceiving Awareness

Part I examines four kinds of supernatural experiences:

- Those in which accurate information comes to us unexpectedly and spontaneously, seemingly out of the blue.
- Those directly but unexpectedly connected to whatever we were thinking at the time.
- Those in which our sense of time and place is altered.
- Those that deliver information to us via our thoughts and feelings, rather than our five physical senses.

Experiences like these can open us to new ways of perceiving the universe and how it interacts with us. These changes in our perceiving awareness are often the first steps in developing our supernatural awareness.

Chapter 2

Out of the Blue

When I was a child, I would talk to God and ask him questions. One day, I was standing in the front yard, and I asked God, "Why aren't people more loving?" Though I was only eight years old, I'd already figured out that you couldn't count on people being nice or kind to you. I couldn't even throw a ball back and forth with a friend without feeling some sense of competition coming from them.

I didn't expect an answer, but immediately after I asked the question, a white pigeon flew down and landed about ten feet from me. I'd never seen a completely white pigeon before, and I knew its appearance meant something. I sensed that my question had been heard and that something unique was occurring—something I hadn't been taught about at home or in school.

My childhood experience with the white pigeon exemplifies a particular type of supernatural experience: one in which there is no clear, easily explainable connection between our own thoughts or actions and something unusual that occurs at nearly the same time. Because they're unexpected, these out-of-the-blue experiences can shake us out of our routine—and out of our current reality.

Recently, I was speaking with a client about animal messages. In many indigenous cultures and shamanic traditions, animals are seen as messengers, and the unexpected appearance of a specific animal is significant. In the spiritual tradition of my Maliseet, Mi'kmaq, and Passamaquoddy grandfather, for example, white birds, like the one I saw as a child, are considered sacred. I said to my client something to the effect that an animal's appearance is significant if it's an animal you don't see all the time, "like your neighbor's black cat or a sparrow." At that moment, a sparrow flew up to the window of my office. It hovered, flying in place as if it were looking in the window. I'd never seen a sparrow do that before, nor have I seen one do so since. That sparrow and my own consciousness were reminding me that creatures that we see every day can give us messages in very unique ways.

Such occurrences may go against your beliefs or what you have learned to expect from your past experience. You might not expect a random animal to be giving you a personal message. You might not expect the world to be so interactive with you in the moment. Unless you were really fortunate enough to have parents or other mentors who were enlightened themselves, the idea of animals as spiritual messengers probably isn't a common viewpoint you would be prepared to embrace.

Such was the case for one of the individuals I interviewed. She was a forty-one-year-old artist of Sioux, Scottish, English, Irish, Danish, and German heritage. She had no history of mental health treatment or substance abuse, and she was atheist.

One day she was leaving an art show opening at a local college. She was feeling upbeat and happy, even giddy, from seeing the artwork. The two glasses of champagne she'd drunk only added to those feelings.

She was getting into her car when she heard her dead German grandmother say to her, clear as a bell, *"Bitte anschnallen,"* which in English meant, "Put your seat belt on." At the same time, she felt as if an unseen force were suddenly pushing her toward these actions.

Her grandmother hadn't been on her mind; the grandmother's voice and the force had just come quickly and out of the blue, with no connection to what she had been thinking or doing at the time. The voice and the force broke through her happy, giddy feelings like a sledgehammer. Immediately and without question, she put her seat belt on.

About fifteen minutes later, as she was driving down the road, she was involved in a car accident. She rolled her car three times. The entire windshield caved in, coming within an inch of her face and throat. It had folded in half and would have sliced her head off if she hadn't been buckled in. When a police officer came to the scene, he shook his head and said something about how she was blessed and very, very lucky. Her only injury was a laceration to her elbow.

Afterward, this woman began to question what had taken place. She had always been an atheist, not a religious person. She didn't believe in an afterlife. She was pretty skeptical. Her first reaction was, "No way. This event could not possibly have been my grandmother saving me." She thought her mind was playing tricks on her.

As time passed, however, she could not deny the evidence. It took her years, but the experience had been so real that she eventually came to believe that her dead grandmother really had put her hand in the car somehow, and she probably would have been dead had she not put her seat belt on.

She sought out others who had similar experiences. Over time she heard other people say someone deceased had stepped in and kept them going, shook them awake, or said, "Don't give up." The more she heard others' encounters and read similar stories, the more she began to believe her grandmother had saved her life that night. Since then, she had become more and more spiritual and now believes that our energy goes on after our physical death. Her experience with the supernatural and how she sought to make sense of it changed both her life and her view of the world.

A different unexpected supernatural experience helped another woman I interviewed through an important life event and transition. She was a twenty-four-year-old, married housewife who'd graduated with a bachelor of arts degree. She was delivering her first child, and because of issues with her pregnancy, the delivery could possibly become dangerous to her and her infant's health. Her doctor asked her husband to make a choice: if the medical staff had to choose whether to save his wife or the baby, what should they do? He chose to prioritize his wife.

During the delivery, the woman went in and out of consciousness, and during that time she saw an apparition of her grandmother. It was the first time she'd ever seen an apparition. It was "transparent, like, she could see her grandmother's face clear as day," but it was like her grandmother's "body wasn't there." Her grandmother "appeared solid but not," as she could see through her grandmother, "but not really." This individual could clearly see almost every detail of her grandmother's face or head, but it was like her body wasn't there or was misty. She didn't know how, but she could tell her grandmother "was wearing something like a white robe." Her grandmother's clothing was "odd, just a long robe-type thing." Her grandmother "was standing beside her bed but not really touching the ground." She didn't know if her grandmother "was all there or not," but she remembered "looking down at the ground, and there were no feet."

Her grandmother's apparition created unknown physiological responses in this woman's body. Her hand where her grandmother's hand had touched it was extremely cold. The feeling of that icy touch on her hand roused fear because she had never experienced this feeling of ice cold before.

When her grandmother talked, "her voice wasn't loud but a whisper." The woman was not too sure if her grandmother had meant to whisper or not. Her grandmother's voice "was audible, like someone in your ear whispering," but her grandmother was a good two, maybe three feet away from her ears. Her grandmother also "didn't move her mouth like normal people do when they talk." She heard her grandmother's voice, but it was hard for her to grasp what she was saying because her grandmother wasn't moving her mouth. Her voice "was like telepathy." She remembered thinking her doctors must have had her "seriously drugged or something, but no drugs had been used because they didn't want to hurt her baby."

Her grandmother told her that "everything would be good," meaning that her doctor would be able to save her and her baby. She told her granddaughter that her doctor and nurses had to work very quickly; she saw that if they made one mistake, this woman would be joining her grandmother in the afterlife. Her grandmother said it wasn't yet her time, and she could just work on living to enjoy her child. Her grandmother didn't say too much, but clearly communicated to her that she had to live.

Her grandmother wasn't there for the whole delivery, which took all of twenty minutes. The woman guessed that her grandmother was only there for a minute, but it seemed like a very long time. For her, time halted or suddenly stopped, as if there were an absence of clock time. "All things that were moving seemed to have stood still while my grandmother was there," she said.

Other people or apparitions seemed to be passing or walking through her grandmother's apparition. Her grandmother didn't appear to mind, though. The woman didn't know if those other people were actually living people or other apparitions. She saw them, but not with her eyes; it was more like seeing with her unconscious or that part of the mind that also sees during meditation or other moments of altered awareness. Her mother later told her that she'd had her eyes closed that whole time, and she doesn't recall ever opening her eyes. She could hear things going on around her, but she didn't see anything but her grandmother and the other people going through her grandmother.

Her grandmother "was very graceful, wavering like a flag in the wind," the woman said. Her grandmother had appeared from nowhere and then just faded into thin air when she left. Her grandmother didn't say anything when she left. The woman experienced her grandmother's "misty self just fading, something like water evaporating into steam."

She was scared at first, but felt a great comfort when she realized the apparition was her grandmother. Her grandmother's presence removed her fear. Yet at that time, she also just couldn't believe her grandmother had really been there. This woman questioned her experience, which seemed improper or unsound according to the science of reasoning.

She remembered her grandmother had had a slow and painful death. It had been very traumatic for all of their family, but affected her, the granddaughter, the most, because her grandmother was the person who had taken care of her growing up. She had been happy to see her grandmother again.

Ever since then, this woman has frequently seen her grandmother watching over her. She knows she communicated with her grandmother. She told her mother that she had seen her grandmother. Her mother didn't believe her at first. But her mother believes her now because she eventually saw her grandmother too.

Unimagined, out-of-the-blue happenings that change our way of experiencing everyday life often involve emergencies and traumas that cannot be replicated. They often occur as part of life-threatening or life-altering circumstances, as they did for the women in the previous two cases. The messengers that appear are usually intimately connected to us in some way. Deceased loved ones with distinct characteristics can respond to our experiences. I believe this suggests that those characteristics are in existence somewhere and can somehow still interact with us even though the loved ones who possessed those characteristics no longer exist on this earth.

Many people who have out-of-the-blue supernatural experiences question the validity of their perceptions, but the outcome is self-evident: their lives are changed significantly in some way by the event, and those changes are demonstrated in the ways the individuals live differently. This dynamic of questioning the event yet changing as a result is *subjective truth*. Someone has a direct, meaningful interaction with extraordinary influences or things, and although the individual has no evidence to verify the interaction as genuine, or a second witness to verify it, the interaction causes a positive outcome for this individual or their life. Subjective truth arises when someone receives information that proves to them that something has happened, yet information is unobtainable via the typical ways of perception. The individual receives an accurate perception of a future event or some other aspect of existence in a way they normally cannot. They then seek validation from others, to find out whether others have had similar experiences.

Reflections: Although it is often good to plan and use practical steps to achieve your life goals, don't forget that some things happen out of the blue. Opening to the idea of these unexpected experiences will lead you to not only new possibilities in your life, but also open your supernatural awareness and more diverse ways of perceiving.

Unexpected events, gifts, and encounters with unusual beings can alter your life for the better. They can symbolically or literally herald a change. For example, a stranger could provide knowledge that helps you avoid a problem situation, or a distant relative could leave you an inheritance.

If you're experiencing a problem, realize there's a chance you might find a solution you never expected or imagined possible. A well-meaning therapist I knew tried to help a teenager whose cat had died. To convince her client the cat was indeed dead, the therapist took a picture of the young woman "pretending" to hold the cat in her arms. The resulting photo, however, clearly showed both the teenager and her cat!

Step away from your point of view to see the situation differently. I remember when many people, including some psychics, had told me my uncle, who had died in World War II, was watching out for me. I thought maybe that wasn't true. But then right as I was thinking those thoughts, I bought a can of soda in a convenience store and received a rare war nickel as part of my change. I immediately recognized I should hold off on making judgements or decisions about my dead uncle's protection until I had more information.

Exercises: Spend a little time on each of the following three exercises:

Make a list of unexpected events that could have or that have changed your life in a positive way.

When you see an unusual animal or an animal in an unusual setting, pay attention to what you were thinking or experiencing just prior to seeing it or as you saw it.

When you receive an unexpected communication (a card or letter, an e-mail, a phone call, or a text) from someone close to you, notice what you were just experiencing prior. Was their message related to the very thing you were just experiencing or thinking about before receiving it? Keep a record of such occurrences. Instead of immediately dismissing the overlap between those communications and your experience/thoughts as coincidental, could you open to other possible explanations?

Chapter 3

The First Thought That Comes into Your Mind

When unforeseen thoughts and images pop into your mind, it can be difficult to tell if they're indications of a supernatural experience. Even if they are, they can come from multiple possible sources. Are you receiving thoughts from supernatural beings, such as entities, aliens, or different beings, angels, or God? Is your soul traveling through an alteration of space and time? Are you using psychic abilities such as clairvoyance, clairaudience, or telepathy? The basic question is, how do you come to know something you are not supposed to know, having perceived it by means other than your basic five senses and that defy the logic of science and reason? It can be tricky to determine whether the first thought that comes to your mind has a natural or supernatural origin. You are perceiving at a level where you are not even aware of taking in knowledge, much less where that knowledge came from or how you took it in.

Supernatural experiences are often validated by external, real-world means. In other words, you think something, and then something in the physical world immediately echoes what you'd just thought, exactly as you'd preconceived it. One of my clients described one version of this kind of validation this way: "The thought appears in my head as my own thought—just a thought that I think I thought. I'll say the words, and then someone else will say, 'I was just thinking that very thought.'"

I've experienced this kind of supernatural experience several times. In my college years, I once traveled around Salem, Massachusetts, with a girlfriend, and we visited the many Salem witch sites. At one of them, tour guides began to tell the story of the many people who were accused of witchcraft and then hanged or imprisoned. One example was a couple, John and Elizabeth Proctor. As the guide said the names, I immediately thought my girlfriend was going to say she was Elizabeth and I was John. Then she said those actual words. I was quite shocked that she had said exactly what my private thought had told me she would.

Years later, after I'd become a therapist, I was conducting a hypnosis session with a research participant. I conducted a hypnosis exercise that followed a particular wording. When I was hypnotizing this man, I kept getting the urge to say, "You think you can open your eyes, but just let them stay closed and relax further." But I didn't say it because I didn't want to alter the wording, which I intended to use for all the research participants. When I interviewed the participant afterward, he said, "I kept thinking I could open my eyes, and I had to stop thinking that thought."

Several people I interviewed in my research for this book experienced the same phenomenon of inexplicable first thoughts coming into their minds. The first was a twenty-six-year-old single male of mixed race and Catholic religion, who was attending a university to obtain his bachelor of arts degree in psychology. He'd had no exposure to the idea of reincarnation or any other alternative religious beliefs.

One day, he was studying with a female friend for a philosophy of ethics test when he looked up and saw her face change into eight different women's faces. The first thought that came into his mind was, "I know those women." Then he thought, "I must be really overtired and working too hard. I'm seeing things." Yet he could not shake his first instant response of recognizing the faces. He didn't mention this internal event to his friend but continued studying.

His initial response bothered him after their study session ended, since he had no proof or way of proving that he'd recognized the women's faces—or even that he'd seen them.

There had been no prior thoughts or events that would have explained why he'd seen these faces. He had never had visions or images so clearly in his mind, except in his dreams or when he was falling asleep or waking up. The images of these faces had appeared during the middle of the day, when he was quite consciously aware. The experience was completely different and alien from any of his past experiences or knowledge. He had never considered the idea of reincarnation, as he was Catholic and believed people had just one lifetime. He did not understand where the thought, "I know those women," would have come from. Several years later he thought, "Could these be the faces of (my friend) in the past lives I had shared together with her?" At the time of the event, he didn't believe in past lives, but later he had an open mind about such possibilities. He could not explain why he saw those faces. He finally laid the issue to rest, concluding that if he'd lived past lives with the female companion he'd been studying with, he would find out someday.

A client of mine from New Hampshire told me of a first-thought experience in which her thought was validated by material evidence. First, she dreamed of a skeleton key to an old home. Then later, while on a business trip, an associate took her to meet a friend, who showed her the exact skeleton key she'd seen in her dream. Seeing in real life the actual skeleton key she'd previously seen in her mind was quite surprising and scary, yet validating for this person.

This next case came from a twenty-two-year-old, married, white, female college student with a bachelor of arts degree and no religious affiliation. She couldn't have been more than ten years old at the time of the experience. Her parents were having a cocktail party with several friends, and one of the female guests was teaching her to dance like Gypsy Rose Lee. She had a lot of fun with this lady. She and this lady connected on many levels, something she had never experienced with an adult before. She had just met her that night, yet she felt she had known this lady her whole life.

As this lady was leaving at the front door, she kissed her on both sides of her cheeks, and the girl "immediately knew this lady was going to die." She knew she would never see her again. Within a few months, this lady was out to dinner with her husband. The lady choked to death on a piece of steak right there in that restaurant and died. The girl told her parents she had known this lady was going to die before she had died.

She said this experience "freaked me out as bizarre" and created heightened emotions within her. She shook off this experience as if it were the opposite of what was expected. She hadn't seen this lady's actual death; she'd just had an overwhelming knowledge that this lady was about to die. She had known and said to herself, "I'll never see her again." The overwhelming knowledge was something she couldn't explain. She just knew, like it was a voice inside of her. She guessed that you could call it a "voice." There was no vision of this lady, but she knew the lady was going to die, "for sure," as if she had an ability to perceive future events. She couldn't explain how she knew this lady was going to die. She had felt dread. She felt a permanent ending of something, a disappearing, and felt deep sadness of a loss.

For her, just knowing yet not knowing how she knew was an interesting idea to explore. Is it possible that she had picked up on a fairly random event (the lady choking to death on a piece of steak) that was somehow a part of that person's energy field or being?

I've heard similar stories from others. A woman told me her story of being home alone at night and having this sense that there was something wrong. She knew someone close to her was in some sort of negative experience, and there was a surrounding sense of a lot of food. She called her fiancé and told him her feelings. He responded, "Are you following me? I was just assaulted outside a restaurant."

Another woman I interviewed—a thirty-two-year-old, divorced, Caucasian female with a high school diploma and no religious affiliation—described an event during which she had the instant thought that her friend's husband was going to kill her friend. She tried to not acknowledge that thought, since, she said, there was no logical support for it. She had never met her friend's husband nor had any reason to know he might ever hurt her friend. He did kill his wife—this woman's friend— several weeks later.[2]

Rather frequently I hear from people who have experienced private inner thoughts or seen images in their mind, and then they experienced these thoughts and images in accurate worldly experiences in their daily lives. There are so many examples to support this point that it is hard to know which to choose. Here are just two.

Once, when I was an undergraduate in college, I was doing a self-hypnosis session, and in my mind's eye I saw woman I had never seen before. I also saw a scene from Colorado with a motorcycle and a sidecar. A little while later, I went out to get a cup of coffee, and there was the same woman from my self-hypnosis, sitting on the porch of my apartment building, reading a newspaper at dusk. She did not live in the building, and I had never seen her before. I felt unsettled. I could not believe it was possible the woman I'd envisioned in my self-hypnosis was now sitting in front of me. I left the building, but while I was getting my coffee, I talked myself into saying hello to her when I returned. However, she was gone when I came back to the apartment, and I never saw her again.

In another example, Kelly Griffin, a co-host for an Internet radio talk show on spirituality, was thinking about an upcoming show with me about my previous book, *Perceptual Hypnosis*, as she was in her car, running errands. She could not remember my last name. She looked up at the closest street sign and saw that the name of the street as she was driving on was Woodard Lane. This sign helped her remember my last name. She perceived that street sign as a supernaturally placed memory trigger.

Many people get impressions, thoughts, and images, and it later becomes evident that they had picked up on things in some way not quite understood by current science. Many people seem to intuit things, events, and human experiences that are beyond the range of their everyday mind.

Here's yet another example from one of the people I interviewed. This person was a sixty-two-year-old, divorced, Caucasian, female medical assistant of Catholic faith. Her oldest brother had recently passed away. As she was driving to her brother's home, ready to clean his apartment, for some reason she thought about a movie called *A Knight's Tale*. She'd always wanted to get that movie on DVD. She had no idea why she was thinking about this movie. But as she was driving down the highway, that movie just popped into her mind. She wasn't thinking about anything else beforehand. Her mother was at her brother's apartment when she arrived. She said, "We will start with trying to clean the closet." And as she opened up the closet door, the DVD of this movie, *A Knight's Tale*, nearly fell on her head.

That movie had been sitting on the shelf, and as she opened the closet, that movie slipped and fell on the floor. She just thought, "That was really strange. Why am I thinking about this movie and here it is?" Her brother had a bunch of DVDs on that shelf, and there was *A Knight's Tale*. She thought that occurrence was a little bit strange, occurring as it did on the day she was going to her brother's apartment, within a week after her brother had died. She felt like her brother had something to do with the movie falling off the shelf.

A variation of this first-thought phenomenon is when our thoughts show us an object and then it actually appears. There are various different ways thoughts can influence our physical environment. One person I interviewed told me, "I just think about something and put a sufficient amount of emotion behind that thought or object. I then don't think about that object or thought anymore. And all of the sudden the object will appear or manifest in my life." I remember one time that I meditated on money and resources, only to find pennies thrown all over my front steps the next morning. Were the pennies a coincidence or strange synchronicity? It was the only time it ever happened in my life.

A forty-two-year-old French and Native American woman I interviewed provided another example. She was a musician and claimed to be able to affect electronic devices. After our initial interview, my microphone and tape recorder went dead. Then we had a follow-up interview on the telephone, and I used the speakerphone because I couldn't locate a new microphone for the new tape recorder I'd bought. After that interview, my telephone stopped working, and I had to purchase a new one. And I was unable to transcribe our second interview because the second tape recorder stopped working.

In that final interview, this woman talked about having an orb of some sort touch her before a number of unusual events started happening around her. She thought the orb was of extraterrestrial origin.

I have never had the problems with my electronic equipment that I did in this situation. My equipment might break down once in a while from use, but all of the pieces have not broken down at once. There was definitely something unusual happening between this woman's internal psychic energy and the electrical and telecommunications equipment in her presence. Everything that happened to my equipment may have been a coincidence, but to me it seemed like more. I think this woman may have been telekinetic or there was some exchange of energy between her being and the electronic objects. At the very least, the experience was interesting. And my mind is open to possibilities. If we can't trust our experience as human beings, how are we to effectively live in the world?

This musician who affected electronic devices told the following story. A neighbor who lived a few doors down from her wanted to hear a song on her album. She told her neighbor that she was not busy, so her neighbor could come over to her apartment. Her neighbor came down, and then the musician said she had to turn on her equipment. She went to get the remote control to turn her equipment on. This remote didn't work. She was kind of angry that her equipment didn't work because she didn't want to disturb her neighbor again. She started pressing the buttons by hand.

Her neighbor said, "Is this equipment plugged in?"

She said, "Yeah, my equipment is plugged in."

Her neighbor said, "Well, I'll have to come another time." Her neighbor said she had to go feed her cat. She was getting hungry as the time was close to lunch.

The musician said, "Wait a minute, I'll play around some more."

All of a sudden, her equipment came on. So then she got her CD. She pressed a button, and a door (to the CD player) opened. There were, like, five openings on this CD player. When she opened one slot, she saw a (John) Lennon CD first, Barry Manilow second, and someone else third. She was trying to find an empty slot. She pushed the button to clear those slots, so she could find a blank opening to put her CD on. She had to rotate through those slots a couple of times until she got a blank one out.

This woman was stooping down with her CD changer in one hand, while her CD was in her other hand. Finally, she found an empty slot and dropped her CD into it. As soon as she dropped her CD in, this CD just vanished. She couldn't believe it had disappeared. This CD had left her fingers and never hit that slot. She got really scared, because that was her first copy. Her other copies hadn't come in yet. She was going to frame this first copy, which was very special to her. She didn't want to lose that CD. She was "a little angry and then a little scared" because she was thinking, what if her keys disappeared or her glasses disappeared?

Her neighbor also got a little scared. The reason she was scared? She was afraid that she was going to disappear, because it happens so often. The woman said her neighbor "was scared like when you have a nightmare and you wake up." Her neighbor backed off and said, "You have some kind of force around you."

Because she couldn't believe her CD had disappeared, she went and got a flashlight. Getting down on her knees, she looked to see if her CD had gotten stuck in the CD compartment.

Her neighbor said, "That's impossible. There's no sunken slot to go into the back of this stereo cause there is really no opening. There's nowhere this CD can go." Her neighbor added, "Maybe it went to heaven."

Then the woman shined her flashlight downward to see if her CD had slid down. She didn't know why she did that, but she did, and then she got "real scared."

"That's my only copy," she said.

Two minutes later, her CD reappeared.

Her neighbor looked, saw it, and took off.

"Wait a minute, I'm going to put this CD in, and you're going to listen to this CD," the woman said.

Her neighbor didn't even wait. "No, I have to go," she said. Her neighbor left and never came back.

On another day, she ran into this same neighbor in the hall.

"You know, if you have time, you can stop by," she said to the neighbor.

"No, I have other things to do," the neighbor replied.

"It would only take a minute. I can switch this CD to track nineteen, and you can listen to the song."

"No, I'm busy."

"Maybe another time." She then asked if her neighbor had a CD player, but she didn't.

Then her neighbor said, "There's something weird—some kind of force, like an energy field, magnetic, or electrical field. Some other people told me some stuff, like you knew someone was going to knock at the door. You described the person, and you weren't even finished and the person was at the door knocking. You're spooky." By spooky, the musician said, the neighbor meant scary—that the musician was someone to be afraid of.

She figured that her neighbor thought she was causing these things to happen, like electricity was coming from her. Like she draws the electricity out of stuff and puts it into other stuff. Like she draws energy out of flashlights.

She hadn't had her neighbor in her apartment to listen to her CD since this event.

Another example of material things being influenced by thoughts comes from the Country Tavern, a Nashua, New Hampshire, restaurant believed to be haunted. A waitress who worked there before it closed in 2020 said, "We (she and a friend) were standing in the (waitstaff) station. There was a shelf with probably twenty coffee cups in it. We were just talking. All of a sudden one coffee cup came flying off the shelf and smashed on the wall in between our two heads. My friend had pottery in her hair. Scared the living daylights out of both of us. We're like, what the heck is that?"

Yet another example comes from a third cousin of mine, who has had streetlights go out when she passed under them and lights in her bedroom turn off in unexplainable ways. Normal explanations were ruled out. These events would occur when she was emotional or upset due to some difficult life situations. These experiences suggest that invisible influences we are not accustomed to recognizing are operating in everyday life.

This type of situation, where you think or perceive something and that occurrence then happens as you envisioned, or your physical environment is affected, points to a deeper reality than just the material or physical view where your consciousness is trapped. These moments of clear awareness seem to come and go, offering glimpses of something much more profound. Your physical world appears to be part of a greater universe.

Such events are not explainable with logic. An individual just knows the words that someone will say before someone tells them or knows what's going to happen before it does. These occurrences are typically out of character for the person experiencing them. They shock the person into new territory, and the person becomes like a pioneer who has seen snow for the first time and now has to describe snow to people who have never experienced it. Some people will believe them. Others will call them liars or say they just imagined snow until they too experience snow. This knowing that the snow experiencer had and these others lacked is not shared. The others' negative responses do not mean snow doesn't exist; rather, the responses mean that they are unable to open up their perception to the possibility to snow.

Such experiences instantly demonstrate that information is being communicated in a way that is different from what we have been taught, as if we have touched some other dimension or reality. You think something, then it happens without you having any prior knowledge to justify your awareness about it beforehand. The probabilities of this type of precognition are not wish fulfillment since you never thought such a thing would occur. And the event is not chance since it is not something that just happens normally in your life.

In trying to understand how this phenomenon manifests, you may try to make more connections between thoughts and events. In an attempt to have another experience like this, sometimes you make connections where there are none, but then realize your mistake since there is no validating evidence after the thought or image. For example, I remember a research subject showing me a video and picture of what he saw as an alien holding a heater with a light at the end. However, the alien, heater, and light were just reflections on an open car door. There are also just coincidences. For example, I remember housesitting for friends when I was in college and watching reruns of the original *Star Trek* while I was studying there. During one episode, I heard Captain Kirk tell Scotty to turn off the power to the *Enterprise* engines, and suddenly, at the same time, the power in the whole house shut off. Obviously, I did not cause a power outage nor did Captain Kirk or Scotty. It was just a strange coincidence. There are times things just happen.

But when all logical explanations can't account for your event, you cannot deny that something happened just the way it did. You are not out of touch with reality, because this event really happened and was validated in your world of living beings, things, and happenings. You were also not a cause of the event because you thought or dreamt about it before it happened. You were aware that something out of your control was happening or would happen, whether you had actual knowledge of it or not. Yet others who have not had these types of experiences, or have not observed them if they have happened, will deny such events can even occur.

Maybe your prior awareness (first thought) has something to do with certain kinds of connections. You may have always thought that your thoughts came from past experiences, from reading your environment, or from asserting power in your environment. But prior awareness is different; the surrounding influence just expanded. The idea that your thoughts can create events or influence things around you is appealing to many but scary and terrifying to others. To complicate matters further, are your thoughts and perceptions maybe able to tell you about things that have happened in the past that you have no way of knowing about? Could they also perhaps tell you what is to come? This mysterious interaction between thoughts and the real world occurs in daily life at various levels.

Can you tap into levels of information that you are unaware of and are not a part of the everyday common knowledge you've been taught? Worse, is the ability to do so innate but socially programmed out of you? How do you perceive something that has not happened yet exactly the way that event later happened? Do you carry the history of all humankind, your ancestors, and possibly even your past lives as if they were part of your true essence or soul, like a movie that you can view for moments at a time? Sometimes random thoughts suggest that we may carry our future with us also.

Perhaps you have an ability to know what is ahead in your life—in events, places, and people. In his book *An Experiment with Time*, J.W. Dunne demonstrated such a talent. At the beginning of the twentieth century, he recorded his dreams and, soon after, noticed correlations between the images in his dreams and events in his everyday life.[3]

Trusting your intuition is important, as your inner experience guides you through the trappings that surround you and that may either expand or restrict you. Misperception restricts your actions and movements and thwarts opportunities in your life. But accurate perception allows you to move through the world safely.

Reflections: Remember that a first thought that comes to your mind as if from nowhere, with no previous connections, can be a divine inspiration, intuitive knowledge from your unconscious mind, or whispers from other beings and places. Breaking free of old chains and blockages created by false knowledge and learning is like removing weeds from your garden so that flowers and vegetables can grow and prosper. It's creating new nerve pathways in your brain while allowing old outdated pathways to atrophy and disappear.

Guiding moments and thoughts occur in unknown ways. For example, an external object, being, or event may point to an opportunity on its way to you. A messenger cannot give you a message unless you understand the implication of that message or the meaning of its appearance.

Exercise: Contemplate the following questions:

1. Have you ever wanted to buy something, but hadn't mentioned it to anyone, only to have someone give you that very thing as a gift? How did the person who gave it to you know you wanted it?
2. Has someone ever said something to you in passing and then what they said came to pass in just that exact way?
3. When you suddenly think something so different from your current train of thought, how do you know the origins of such a thought? What constellation of things brought that new thought into your supernatural awareness?

For example, I'd never seen an otter on the waterway by my property. Yet one day I had the thought that I should move to a more remote place where I could see otters. Soon after having that thought, I saw an otter on my property while I was walking my dog. A logical person would say I was looking for an otter and just didn't notice any otters there before. However, I had always searched for them when walking in that area. I know the appearance of the otter was a message saying that what I need will present itself wherever I am.

I had another otter experience when I was doing some exploratory hypnosis with a lay hypnotist. She was teaching me hypnosis and attempting to explore my past lives and my Native American connections. I had some imaginary and creative thoughts that were important: I saw two otters playing in a river. The image was as real to me as sitting next to someone and talking to them in the physical world. I later learned that in the traditions of my Maliseet, Mi'kmaq, and Passamaquoddy ancestors the otter was the animal associated with my birth sign. But I did not know this at the time I saw the image. I received subjective validation for my thought after the fact, when I stumbled on knowledge that verified it. That validation signaled that the original thought was a meaningful message for me.

Chapter 4

Altering Time and Space

Some supernatural experiences seem to bend the rules of time and space—or at least, what we *think* those rules are. Conversations with dead ancestors, foreseeing future events, losing time during an encounter with a mysterious aircraft, communicating energetically with animals, hearing others' thoughts, and stepping out of the body are just some of the extraordinary experiences that can alter people's points of view, expand their physical limitations in unexpected ways, and change their attitudes about what is true about time and space.

An experience that alters someone's sense of time means that the entire event, or parts of it, doesn't unfold in the logical, sequential order that the person expects and understands to be reality. An experience that alters someone's sense of space means that the entire event, or parts of it, doesn't adhere to what the person understands to be the laws of the physical environment.

Events may occur out of what the experiencer thinks of as a normal time sequence yet are later validated. Events like this can make us wonder whether time really is sequential, whether events can occur out of sequential time, or whether different aspects of time, such as past, present, future, are, in fact, happening simultaneously all at once.

For example, a seven-year-old girl told her mother that she talked to her grandmother and saw this grandmother in her mind. But when her mother showed her a picture of both her grandmothers, the child responded, "Those are not my grandmother." Later, when visiting her uncle's home for the first time, the girl pointed to a picture on the wall and said the woman in it was the grandmother she had been speaking with.

The woman in the picture wasn't her grandmother, but her great-grandmother. Was this young girl talking with a relative from her family's past? Was her great-grandmother talking with a relative three generations forward in her family's future? Were they really talking with each other across time, or were they both talking to one another "live," in what for each of them was the present?

This experience brings up an interesting question: Are unknown people who appear in our dreams and visions truly unknown to us? Or could they, in fact, be people we *do* know but not in our current present time-space reality as we understand it? Say that you see in your mind someone you don't know and then later see them exactly in the same way in the external world. Where did your preconceived image come from? How did those perceptions enter your consciousness before you saw that person in the physical?

On the other hand, in your mind, you may see someone you actually do know, but they appear different from the way they usually appear to you. I remember the first time I saw a picture of my grandmother Teresa Riccardo as a young woman. I would have never recognized her because, in the picture, she looked so different from how I knew her in life (when she was older). In a similar way, someone you may see in a dream or vision can be someone you know, but you don't consciously recognize them because they don't look like the person you know. How could you recognize them if you haven't seen any photos or other evidence telling you how they looked before you knew them in life?

Precognitive visions or dreams, especially, can make us question whether time is the sequential phenomenon we typically think it is. I interviewed a twelve-year-old Caucasian female who reported having a dream that included a broken chair. She didn't know how the chair had broken or what made it break. The next morning, her mother was trying to change a burned-out light bulb in an outdoor light fixture at her family's home. Her mother was standing on a chair. Below the light fixture was a set of steps; to one side of the steps was a bush, and there were flowers and a tree on the other side. This girl's friend was outside the house too. The girl had gone back inside the house to get a screwdriver from a closet when she heard her mother fall off the chair. Her mother made a noise, "uh," when she fell. The girl ran outside to see what was going on and saw her mother sitting down on the ground. She also saw that the chair her mother had been standing on, which had been placed close to the steps, had fallen down. It had broken and was laying on its back in the dirt—in the same exact position as the girl had seen it in her dream the night before. She recognized it as the same chair because the legs were slanted, just like those of the chair in her dream.

Another person I interviewed, a twenty-three-year-old, single Caucasian male, also shared a precognitive dream he'd had as a teenager. He had no religious affiliation, was unemployed, and had an eighth-grade education. His dream was more disturbing than that of the young woman who had seen the broken chair. In our interview, he nicely described so many consequences that such a time-bending event can have for an average person.

When he was fifteen years old, he had a dream about his neighbor, whom he had known for probably ten years. He dreamed this male neighbor was outside in winter, walking his black poodle, when he had a heart attack and died. The young man could see his neighbor lying on his back. His neighbor was lying in the street, exactly where it had been plowed, right next to a snowbank and a rose bush. He was holding the poodle's brown leash, and the poodle was going around sniffing his neighbor's body. There wasn't anyone else there.

In the dream, the young man was trying to think why he was the only one who could see his neighbor. In the dream, this event had occurred during early evening, and there was still light, so it didn't make any sense that no one else could see his neighbor's body. But there wasn't any movement. He couldn't hear anyone.

He later told his parents about the dream and said he thought the dream was an omen or a foreshadowing of the future. They did not disbelieve him, but he didn't think they gave a lot of credence to the idea of his dream being a true vision of the future until his neighbor actually did have a heart attack and died a week later. Then they acknowledged his dream as a valid vision of future events. They were astonished or dumbfounded, but their minds opened to the possibility that future events can sometimes be foreseen.

In our interview, this man recalled the actual day of his neighbor's death and his reaction to it. When the ambulance came, he was outside, playing with some children in the snow. He remembered running to see where the ambulance had gone, and he saw that it was at his neighbor's house. He ran back to his parents' house to tell them an ambulance was there. The emergency medical technicians took the neighbor to the hospital, along with his wife, but brought only her back to the house. Indeed, his neighbor had died. He had died in his bed, but the doctors figured out that he had actually had a heart attack while he had been outside earlier, walking his dog. Then he had gotten back home, where he died quite rapidly.

Because of the dream, this young man had been sure his neighbor was going to die of a heart attack. When his neighbor did die a week later, he remembered, he had been very scared and shocked. He realized that what he had seen in his dream had really happened—almost exactly the way he'd dreamed it. He said the event itself was quite disconcerting, almost kind of surreal. Although he wasn't there, in his neighbor's house, he could see everything that was going on. He just knew his neighbor's death was occurring, and he was just very scared to know about something before it happened. He was scared because he couldn't explain how he had known his neighbor was going to die in that way.

This occurrence was quite disconcerting for someone so young. His neighbor's death hadn't seemed like a very long part of his dream, but this dream had woken him up on the night he'd had it. On that night, he was kind of in shock at the idea of someone he knew dying. He didn't have any experience with death at that point in his life. At first, he had been relieved to realize his vision of his neighbor's death had only been a dream, but later, when his neighbor actually had a heart attack and died, he was upset.

On the night of the dream, when he had woken up, it felt like his neighbor's death had actually happened. He told me he had been in that state when you wake up from a dream and are not sure if that dream actually occurred or you were still dreaming, because you are kind of groggy. He had woken up and thought, "Sure, it happened" —meaning, he had gotten the impression his neighbor's death already had happened, although it actually hadn't. He felt like he had just seen his neighbor's death. That's why he woke up in that state.

His neighbor's death had just been so, so clear. The whole clarity of the event was just quite shocking.

On the day his neighbor actually died, he didn't know why he knew his neighbor had died of a heart attack. The neighbor's death could have been due to an aneurysm or other medical conditions he didn't know about. Yet he just knew it was a heart attack, and had no idea how he knew. There was no doubt within him. The way he knew wasn't visual or anything like that; it was just an absolute knowing of knowledge that he couldn't be expected to know. He had this visual picture of his neighbor lying on his back, and then what he had was just knowledge. He absolutely knew his neighbor's death was due to a heart attack, without question. Even more bizarre was that his neighbor was a very healthy guy in his early seventies, always working outside, very physically fit. You would not have expected him to have a heart attack. The young man had just had a feeling of knowledge—an absolute knowing. That's the best way he could explain the experience: some kind of knowledge comes to you, and you know is true as soon as it comes. As soon as it appears, there is no doubt.

He was scared that he'd known those things before the events happened. He recalled in the interview that at the time of his neighbor's death he felt scared. He said he also still felt scared because of this experience he'd had as a teenager. He didn't want to know things in advance; knowing it might happen again caused him stress. First, the dream itself had been stressful: the stress was like adrenaline in his body, and it altered his breathing when he woke up, as if he'd actually seen his neighbor die. Second, he hadn't wanted to have that vision, and he couldn't have blocked it out. He didn't want to know bad things would happen before they did. He didn't want to know things in advance when he couldn't prevent them from happening. He just didn't want prior knowledge of some horrific events.

He had no way of explaining how he could have had a precognitive dream of someone's death. This was his first experience of that type. He told me, you are taught to believe you cannot see those things. So when you do, you are taught to believe you are crazy because these things cannot occur. It is not logical. Yet when he'd had his dream, he had known that this neighbor's death was going to happen. He was stressed out for a few months afterward. He didn't want to have dreams that later came true because he has bad dreams a lot.

Society tells you if you are thinking anything not from your logical mind, you are wrong, he said. Any changed sequence of events cannot be possible, so you start to think that you are insane. He did not want to think he was illogical or insane. That was pretty scary.

Seeing potential future events is only one way a supernatural experience may challenge our understanding of time. Some people have reported traveling to the future. A woman with a master's degree in archaeology told me about a dream in which she had done just that. She said that in the dream she was taken by "something higher than an angel to the year 3000 and something." She saw people sleeping together in sleeping bags in one room of a house, as if they were trying to hide or to protect each other. A form of supernatural authority figures — not police but guardians — came because she was not supposed to be there and awake in that room. These guardians gave her an injection with a futuristic instrument. The injection hurt, and the pain took her out of that dream. She also went to the year 4000 or later in another dream, but didn't see any life there.

A slightly different time alteration happened in the case of an "energy vampire" whose full story appears in Chapter 9. He reported leaving his body and traveling to visit people he knew. Sometimes these people told him that he had appeared to them at a much later time than he had perceived in his understanding of time.

No examination of altered time would be adequate without addressing missing time. Especially in alien abduction cases, this is a prevalent phenomenon. This next case describes a middle-aged Caucasian woman's experience of missing time.

On a Sunday in February, her husband, who she said had always been a super early bird, was up, and he was looking out the window. He saw weird lights. He came in the bedroom and said, "Mary, get up. Come on and come look at these weird lights out here." She fell back to sleep, so her husband came in the second time, saying, "Mary, hurry up! You are going to miss these lights. Get up." So she jumped up and went into her kitchen to the window. She remembered looking at her microwave, and the clock time was 4:12 in the morning. She also remembered swearing in her head because her husband had woken her up at four o'clock in the morning. But as soon as she looked out the window, she woke up fully.

She saw this black triangle that was not normal. She became wide awake. By "wide awake," she meant that she had gotten out of bed, woken up, and was kind of groggy a little bit. For her, seeing that triangle woke her right up.

Surprised and shocked, she said, "Gosh, what the hell is that?"

To her, this thing looked like two big headlights on a truck or a car, and it was on the horizon. These weird lights were unusual white lights. Her husband saw bigger white lights, not those of an airplane. He saw three lights on the points of this black triangular object.

She and her husband lived by the airport. The airport would have been to her right as she was looking out the window. But this object was to her left, on the horizon. She was so surprised, looking at this object, and then she and her husband went out on the porch to get a better view, which she thought later was probably stupid. She assumed and thought to herself later that if she and her husband hadn't gone out on their porch, they wouldn't have experienced any missing time.

She went out onto her porch and was standing in front of the stairs, with her husband in front of her, and she wrapped her arms around him. She could feel her husband's heart pounding, and she remembered saying, "Carl, go get your phone." She was whispering at him. He said, "I can't move." (Her husband was telling her to shut up in a nice way.) She could feel that her husband was scared, and she was scared, so she was trying to make him feel at ease a little bit.

She said, "Oh, honey, this object is probably military. There's a base, and the airport is right there."

He said, "That's not military."

The next thing she remembered, she was standing by the outside table that was to her right, which was weird. But those tables were right next to her. She had her arms out and down, and she was looking up. She could see this object was going right overhead, and it was a huge black triangle. She remembered there were grates underneath this black triangle. She could feel a warmth, which she thought was maybe caused by a motor part because there was a humming or buzzing—a swishing-type sound. She had never heard anything like this humming and buzzing before in her life. It was hard to describe or put into words. "You open your mouth and just blow," she said. "That's what it sounded like." Yet the surroundings were unusually quiet—no wind, no birds, no noise, nothing at all, nothing. She remembered two or three tiny, tiny red lights underneath this triangle. She didn't think these lights were blinking. This black triangle object wasn't even fully overhead.

She remembered looking at her husband; she turned and looked at him.

Then she kind of shook things off a little bit. She described herself as robotic and not herself. Her husband wasn't himself either. She remembered her head being back and her arms being up; her arms were out to her side. She clearly remembered feeling herself putting her arms back down to her waist. In her mind, she remembered thinking that seeing that object was weird to her. She had this thought even before that craft was fully gone from their view but was still right over her head.

She looked over at her husband and said, "You saw what I saw." And he said, "Yup, you saw what I saw." Then they just walked into their house. Her husband looked at her. He went to the computer, and she went to the TV. And they were quiet and did not talk with each other. After thinking about and processing her and her husband's reactions, she thought their responses seemed very robotic.

When she had seen that triangle or craft originally, she remembered thinking that it was dark out. She remembered seeing that triangle through a big pine tree, and then there were a couple of dead trees, and she could see the craft over these trees. She could have thrown a rock at that triangle craft. But the sky had started to get dark, so she could not make out if there was something in the sky or those trees. Afterward, in the house, recalling what she'd seen, she sat in her chair and thought, "Well, wait a minute. It was jet black outside, dark, and now it's kind of light." So she moved from where she was resting to look at their clock on the microwave. That clock's time was 4:47 a.m.

She was shocked and wondered, "Who do you call when you go through something like that?" Once when she was a young girl, she had seen a balloon in the sky, and she had watched where that balloon went. She had watched the triangle/craft in a similar way. Yet she and her husband hadn't watched where that black triangle object, something that huge, had gone. Instead they had just walked into the house. She thought this was not a normal reaction, given the circumstances.

Her husband used to be very much into UFOs—always watching shows about them, looking stuff up. The next day or so after he and she had seen the craft, her husband made a report to the Mutual UFO Network (MUFON) or another UFO-sighting group. She had called her mother-in-law, thinking she was crazy after her experience. That black triangle object was just not something that you see every day—or actually ever, really. She didn't feel that she was crazy or that she ever went crazy. She said that, in reality, she just wanted confirmation that her experience had happened and other people have witnessed events of this type.

She next contacted a paranormal research group. "Who should I call when something like this occurrence happens?" she had wondered, and she had Googled "paranormal" on her smart phone. She believed it was not appropriate to call the police. This paranormal group came out to their house and had her and her husband fill out a questionnaire. She found them helpful.

What causes one to miss time? Is it the shock of such an unusual experience, such as being abducted, placed on an unknown craft, and seeing beings that are not human? Are the experiencers dissociating and placing their experience at low levels of awareness? I remember hypnotizing a woman who had experienced an alien abduction. I asked her to leave her body and view from a distance what had been going on during the abduction. By stepping outside herself, she would be able see what happened to her and whom she interacted with. She responded, "They won't let me." It was an interesting response, suggesting that someone was exerting some kind of mental control or influence over her. That external influence may well have been the reason this woman experienced missing time as part of the event.

Another woman I interviewed also reported missing time after seeing an unusual aircraft. She was a thirty-two-year-old Caucasian female, Catholic, with a high school education; a government contractor, she worked as a receptionist. She was driving home from work at approximately 2:00 a.m.

"And I looked up, and that's when I saw this huge craft," she recalled. "I can't even put (it) into words other than to say it was about three football fields in length and about three stories high. And it had, like, colored lights along the bottom of it, and above that was, like, what a second story would be like, it had windows. I say they are like windows because it was, like, a white light illuminating out of them. Then the rest of these windows were just as gray as the sky, and all you could see was, like, an outline. I think it must have been a moonlight or something."

After seeing the craft, she realized she was still in her car, but that the time was now about 3:05 a.m. She had missed about an hour of time.

The next day, her six-year-old daughter asked her about the beautiful lady she had seen in her mother's room the night before. Her daughter reported that this lady had had blonde hair and blue eyes, and she was "wearing something they wear on *Star Trek*." The daughter said she had tried to wake up her mother, but she couldn't. The woman had no recollection of this lady being in her bedroom.

This woman's experience with the mysterious aircraft was later validated, as others reported seeing a similar object in the sky that same evening.

Supernatural experiences can play with our sense of not just time, but also physical space. Communicating across great distances without mechanical devices—and even without words—is a phenomenon that can challenge what we think are the typical limitations of the physical realm, as the next case demonstrates. The individual who shared it was a thirty-six-year-old woman of Irish, Italian, Turkish, and Native American descent. She was a mother and a Christian, and she had a bachelor's degree.

She had gone to Florida one fall because she was suffering from severe health problems and had arranged for some medical treatment there. She was feeling hopeful that these medical treatments were going to be successful.

While there, she had a couple of days where she did not have to go to doctors' appointments. She decided to go swimming in the ocean. She had lost a significant amount of weight, and she thought she looked like a skeleton. Yet despite her negative perception of her appearance, she went to the beach.

She described her swimming as wonderful, because it was really nice warm water. She moved far enough away from other people in the ocean water that she couldn't hear their conversation. She was far enough from the beach that there was this little red pole sticking out of the water near her. The ocean water was deep, up to her neck, yet she could still touch the sand under the water.

She had recently watched a movie and read articles about dolphins. These sources of information had said that dolphins were super intelligent. Their brains are shaped like our brains, she remembered, and they actually use more of their brains than we use of ours, according to several studies. She was feeling a deep respect and awe for dolphins when she was in the water. She was thinking about how dolphins communicate through song, according to what she had read. To her, their communication was kind of like music. She wanted to sing some dolphins a song. In her singing, there weren't any words; it was more like humming a tune. She was sending her vibration by just singing something that she thought sounded really nice. She was thinking the whole time how she wanted some dolphins to come to her. She was emitting energy, this great feeling of love, toward dolphins.

This woman had always been really in love with nature. She loved the ocean. She loved animals deeply. When she was in the water, surrounded by this beautiful beach, she had hoped that her health was going to get better. Everything about the experience was so beautiful it was overwhelming. She was thinking about the dolphins. She wanted to use her love for nature and life to communicate with some dolphins at that moment. She didn't have any bad feelings at that time. She wasn't worried about anything. She was just one with the earth, just loving being alive, and grateful for life. What she wanted to emit to these dolphins was just peace and love and respect for what and who these dolphins are.

She had been in the water for a little while, and she was getting tired. She wasn't healthy, so she said to herself, "I'm going to go home." Her hotel room was not far away. Anyways, she thought, no dolphins were coming. So after a while, she said to herself, "Well, it's probably time for me to go back to shore." She looked around and didn't see any dolphins near her.

"Well, maybe those dolphins enjoyed my singing anyways," she thought. She stopped floating in the water and began walking back towards that beach.

When she had reached a level of water that was down to her calves, she saw that a bunch of people who had been sitting on that beach, sun tanning, had now stood up. These people were pointing—like, "Oh no!" There was all this uproar. All these people were pointing behind her. They all looked shocked.

She turned around, and there were four to six dolphins in the water by that little red pole she had seen earlier. Some of these dolphins were swimming. Some of them had their heads sticking up out of the water, just looking. Some would go under the water, then pop their heads out, and then go underwater again. She couldn't really tell exactly how many dolphins there were.

"Oh, my God, they came!" she said. Then she said to these other people on the beach, "Wow, when did they show up?"

"They just showed up," the people said.

She wanted to say, "Oh, that's because I called them with my song." But of course, she didn't say that because she didn't want the people on the beach to think she was crazy.

When she was walking up to the people on the beach, there was one girl who stood out to her the most, because this girl was the most excited. She wanted to tell this girl that all these dolphins were here because she had called them. But again, she didn't want this girl to think she was crazy. If somebody comes up to you and tells you she had called these dolphins, that that's why these dolphins are here, some people aren't ready to hear that, or they don't quite understand. A lot of people don't believe in the fact that you can communicate with animals or that there's something more to life than scientific facts. So if she were to go and randomly tell someone she was talking with these dolphins through song, and these dolphins heard her and had come to her, this other person was going to think she was crazy. They can't grasp it, maybe because they haven't experienced it. She didn't know; maybe this other person wouldn't have thought she was crazy. But she just took a safe path and kept that information to herself. She didn't know this girl, and she didn't need to tell her about it.

Later, she told her fiancé and other people she knew would understand her experience. But at the time, she was just so tired that she went home. After a while, these dolphins swam off and disappeared.

This amazing dolphin experience was one she always reflected back on. It really confirmed she had connected and communicated with these dolphins, which were right there next to that red pole. She was amazed by the magic or unexplainable influences and how beautiful this experience was. She couldn't believe these dolphins had actually come to the spot where she had been singing. She wasn't sure if these dolphins had been hanging out underwater for a while (before anyone saw them) or if they had just showed up and were communicating, "Hey, where did you go?" This experience with these dolphins gave her a joy for life, and a sense of knowing that we don't understand everything and life can be so magical. She always thought of this dolphin experience when she was in a lot of pain with her illness. Or in dark times, she remembered these dolphins and how they responded to just love and her singing. Every time she felt like giving up, or just was really struggling with the constant pain of her chronic illness, or wondered why this life is so full of suffering, she thought about these dolphins. Her experience made her realize that there was much she still hadn't experienced in life—things that can happen and defy current analytical reasoning. There was always a little light that came back inside her when she thought about these dolphins. To her, it was just amazing and beautiful how we can communicate with other animals.

Animals can be spiritual messengers, according to several spiritual traditions. So can animals interact with humans in meaningful, supernatural ways? Many people who connect with animals believe they can. A forty-nine-year-old married man shared another example of animal communication—one that happened spontaneously. He was of French-Canadian and Native American descent, and he had chronic disabling back pain. He reported:

> One day I was in particularly bad pain, and I was alone. My wife had left to do something with our work, and my pain was bad. I was just sitting there, crying. I wasn't wailing or anything, but tears were coming out of my eyes.
> My parrot, Ty, backed off my shoulder and looked me right in the face. And then he said, "It's okay."
> It was sort of like a watershed moment. It was more than just the words. The words were his way of relating to me. I guess

when he was in bad shape or he was afraid or something, people had tried to calm him by telling him, "It's okay." It's a natural thing to say, "It's okay. Calm down." He made the connection that I needed to be told that it was okay, that I was going to make it through this situation, and since then, he is sort of like my guardian angel.

Like animal communication, extrasensory communication between humans can challenge our perception of how the physical world supposedly operates. The following example came from a forty-five-year-old, male, Polish artist of Lutheran faith.

"I remember I was in sixth grade in an art classroom," he reported. "I had drawn a picture, and I asked this little girl behind me, 'Oh, do you like my picture?' She said, 'Yes.' But I heard verbally in my head, her saying, 'No, I don't.' I looked at her, and I said, 'Did you just say, *no, I don't*?' She said, 'How do you know that?'"

Such experiences are subjective and unplanned. They are considered supernatural moments as I defined *supernatural* earlier. Since such occurrences are not supposed to happen, they can alter our understanding of the world. They also demonstrate that the majority of our untapped potential remains quite mysterious, but periodically shows itself to us in spontaneous, unexpected ways. These changes in what seem to be the limitations of our physical senses occur during everyday life. How did we learn to perceive these limitations to begin with? And how can we learn to perceive them differently, perhaps seeing them not as limitations at all?

Most people would recognize a place they have never physically visited if they had previously seen it in photos or video. But how might your perception of the physical world change if you discovered you were intimately familiar with a place you had literally never seen—in person or in pictures?

That's what happened to another woman I interviewed. She was eighty years old, retired, married, Caucasian, and a Christian. She had had an unusual experience when she and her husband were visiting Franklin, New Hampshire. Although she had never been there, she told her husband there would be a greenhouse with a white picket fence on a particular street. Sure enough, as they went to that street to see if she was correct, there was the green house with a white picket fence, just like she described. "I just felt like I had been there before," she told me. "But I had never been there."

Unexpected alterations in our interactions with our physical environment can change our understanding of that environment. Another man I interviewed experienced a dramatic shift in perspective while sitting with his wife in their living room on a snowy day. He was forty-two years old, biracial, Catholic, and had a master's degree.

He was looking out the window, and his wife was on her computer. He was content and happy, without any particular thoughts on his mind. Suddenly, as he was looking out the window, he saw an older man, graying and balding, walking around the side of their house. He ran into their kitchen and outside through a sliding door to their porch. He wanted to ask the man what he was doing there. However, when he reached the porch, there was no man, and there were no footprints in the snow. He believed he had seen a discarnate spirit or ghost.

The experience bothered him because he didn't understand why he had seen the spirit of an older man. He doesn't normally see such things. He later came to the conclusion that seeing this man was a way of the universe letting him know such things exist. This experience didn't harm him in any way. He was just frustrated because he couldn't prove to anyone this happened. At the time he talked to me, he hadn't had any other similar experiences.

This man believed he had seen a fellow human being, and he responded as though he had. Upon noticing that there were no footprints in the snow, he realized he must have perceived something quite different from what he thought he had. His perception of his environment was altered, as he had never seen something that did not follow the physical laws of science. Physical beings leave footprints, yet the being he saw did not. So what kind of being was it? How could beings exist without such physical interactions with the environment?

In this next example, an individual had an experience that challenged how she perceived movement in both time and space. This woman was a thirty-year-old registered nurse from New Hampshire. At the time, she was the mother of two young children, who lived at home with her.

She had traveled to Maine to help set up for a baby shower for her sister-in-law. A snowstorm had been predicted that day, but it wasn't supposed to start until about four o'clock in the afternoon. So she had left for Maine about nine o'clock in the morning. The trip was a two-and-a-half, almost three-hour drive. Before the shower, her in-laws expressed concern about her driving home in the coming snowstorm. She told them, "I'll leave soon. As soon as the shower starts, if it starts to snow, I will leave." Lo and behold, the snowstorm didn't really start until after she had left the baby shower.

She didn't remember the times so exactly, but she thought it was around three o'clock when she left to return home. When she reached the Portland area, the falling snow became blizzard-like conditions. Back then, cell phones were not available. She couldn't call and let her family know that she was okay.

As she entered New Hampshire, she was driving very, very slowly. The snow was quite heavy and getting really deep. She couldn't see the road. Apparently, the snow had started falling in New Hampshire before it had started in Maine.

As she drove onto Route 101, she turned on her windshield wipers. Suddenly, her driver's side windshield wiper flew off. So she stopped her car and got out. She did have her coat, hat, and gloves on. But inadvertently she locked the car behind her. Her car was on; the engine was still running. She didn't know what to do, because there were no cars on the road at all. So she went looking where she thought her windshield wiper had gone onto the side of the road. She couldn't really tell if it had gone out in the middle of the road, but she couldn't see anything, so she went to the side. She saw a vehicle coming down the road, but it took the off-ramp exit (before reaching her). Then she didn't see anything for a while.

She had been outside probably at least a good twenty minutes, looking and digging in the snow, because she figured her windshield wiper had just catapulted and could be anywhere.

Suddenly, this truck was in back of her car—a pickup truck, a 4x4-type thing. She had not seen this truck coming. She had not seen its lights. The truck just appeared. She didn't remember the color of this truck. But she remembered there was a man in it. She would say he was probably about twenty-five years old.

He got out of the truck. She remembered that he was wearing a pair of jeans that had a bib, like farmer-type jeans, and he had a shirt on. She had thought he was dressed like it was summer. He did not have a coat on. He was looking around and so forth.

He came over and said, "Can I help you?" She remembered saying to him, "Oh, you must be cold, and you probably need a coat." And he said, "What's the problem?"

She told him what happened—how she had lost her windshield wiper and locked her keys in her car. So he went back to his truck and got what she believed was a hanger. He unlocked her car quickly. Then he helped her find her windshield wiper, finding it in a place where she had already looked. He found her windshield wiper almost instantaneously. He just knew where to go over and look for it. He put her wiper back on her car. He didn't say much to her except, "Have a good day."

She remembered thanking him profusely. She wanted his address. She went back to her car to look for some money in her purse, because she wanted to give him some money for helping her. (She had maybe four to seven dollars with her.) But when she looked back for him, the man and his truck were gone. There were no tire tracks indicating where he had come from and no tire tracks indicating that he had turned around and driven off the other way. There were no tracks showing that he had driven around her and her car. It was snowing, so she would have seen such tracks. He had gone back to his truck, and then he was gone. His truck had just disappeared.

The woman had thought she was in a dream. She remembered looking for and finding no tire tracks, which was bizarre to her but didn't scare her at all. She was covered with snow, so she went back in her car and was like, "What just happened?" Then she thought the man had been her angel that came to help her.

This experience had stayed with her ever since. She said she could still see what happened, just like it was right there—just like his truck was planted there.

This next supernatural event demonstrates the possibility that we can alter what is happening at another location. Influencing people, events, and things at a distance is an interesting phenomenon to contemplate. Such experiences are rare but not unreported. *Please note: this story contains details of an attempted suicide.*

The woman who shared this experience was a twenty-year-old, single, Caucasian college student. The event happened during a night in January, five years before our interview. Her best friend at the time was a guy named Bob. They had been friends about two years, and she said she thought they told each other everything. But her friend had never told her about his depression or his suicidal thoughts.

One night, she drifted off to sleep as usual, but dreamt something that would haunt her for as long as she lived and change both her and her friend's lives forever.

In the dream, she walked into her friend's (Bob's) house. She had been there many times before, but never at night and never in dead silence. She was frightened, but she knew she had to find her friend, to ask him what was going on. She found the doorway that led to the basement. She heard his guitar playing. So she followed that sound and slowly crept down that stairwell.

As she went further down the stairs, she began to look around a wall into the basement. She saw her friend hunched over his guitar, crying, trying to play as if nothing were wrong.

"Bob?" she asked. But no answer came back, as her friend didn't know she was there. She could tell that her friend's pain was all he felt.

She watched as he set down his guitar and walked over to another section of the basement. She raced down the rest of the steps and over to his guitar, only to see his guitar stained with tears. Through the hall, she saw him load a gun, a smaller black handgun, and place it to his head.

She was frightened beyond belief and knew she had to stop him from hurting himself. Her fright was just a gut feeling— "like you have a gut feeling something is about to happen." She just knew in her mind that she had to do something, but she didn't know what. Her gut feeling was really hard to describe. She relies on her feelings a lot. Her feelings in her gut just told her that something was not right there. And in her mind, she knew that something was not right. She had to figure out what was really going on and why she was there.

Still in the dream, she knew she had to do something to save him from that bullet. While she watched him squeeze that trigger, she closed her eyes and screamed his name, "Bob!" A picture of his house flashed in front of her closed eyes, and she heard the sound of a gunshot. These images happened really quickly.

She woke up from the dream screaming and sweating. She was panicked. That dream had been just really real. She felt so much in that dream. When she woke up, she still felt what she had felt within that dream. She felt as if she had witnessed what happened. At the time, she thought she was crazy—not literally, but just like anyone would be, thinking, "It's only a dream."

She loved Bob as a friend, and this dream experience was like seeing one of her good friends going into a suicidal fit. She was panicked and wanted to call him.

One thing was very odd: when she had woken up, the time was 2:59 a.m. She had been born at 2:59 a.m. She didn't know if that detail meant anything.

About a week later, she told Bob what she had dreamt, and he burst into tears. On that night, everything she had seen in her dream actually had taken place, but as Bob had squeezed the trigger of the gun, he had seen her and pulled the gun away from his head. He showed her the burn mark on his neck where the bullet had grazed him and the hole in his basement wall where that bullet entered it.

For her, this experience confirmed that she had "some weird supernatural power." This power was just with her dreaming, like she had described. She could often "feel" when there was something wrong with someone. Through dreaming, she would get images and thoughts of little things that would then happen in the future. For example, during one dream, she saw herself going through her friends' houses. Later, she was able to describe their houses to them, and they would be amazed that she knew how their houses were arranged, though she had never been there. She would also dream about who was going to get into a fight or about something that would happen to her family. She had seen herself at the college she was at now.

She predicted where she would go to school before she even applied.

She had glimpsed events and foreseen such things in the past through dreams, but never something as major as her friend's attempted suicide. To this day, she told me, her friend claims that had she not "been there" with him, he would be dead. Whether she did something or not, she would never be certain. She was glad Bob was still with her as a friend and that she had somehow made an impact on his life. Because of this dream experience, she could now handle a lot of situations most others could not and recognize a suicidal person through just a "feeling" about them.

Out-of-body experiences inherently challenge what we believe to be real about our physical bodies, our consciousness, and our physical environment. This next case was presented by a forty-two-year-old married woman of Irish and German descent and of Catholic faith, who had finished high school. She had been in a major accident in which she was hit by a car and dragged along the road. Her back had been broken, and her jaw was seriously broken. She received fifty-four stitches in her chin.

She reported that as her doctors were working on her mouth and jaw, she floated above her body. She felt no pain and was not scared when she was looking down on her body. She never felt she was going to die.

She remembered the whole process of this doctor working on her mouth. She was lying in her emergency room bed. This medical doctor was giving her a shot in between each tooth. She remembered these shots between her teeth as being painful. At that point, she was totally in her body. Then she was just watching this doctor put the different little procedure things, rubber bands and all the stuff, on her gums.

It was when she was done with these shots that she left her body. She didn't remember the shots being, "Ow, this is painful." Leaving her body happened just all of the sudden, and she was up there, watching her doctor. The light was going down, and he started to put on the apparatuses that he needed. She didn't have any awareness of any pain at that time.

She didn't remember "going up there" and leaving her body either. Suddenly, she was above this bed, in a corner of this room, watching what was going on to her physical body. She had absolutely no pain. She didn't really have feeling in her body; she didn't feel there was a physical aspect to her body.

It looked like there were lights below her, and it was almost like there was no ceiling up where she was looking down from. She could see these lights coming kind of from below her into this room. That was the most significant thing she remembered: how these ceiling lights were down below her. Of course, there was a ceiling there, so her perception of there being no ceiling "just doesn't kind of make sense," she said. But that's the way she perceived those lights.

This woman didn't ever feel scared or like "hanging up there above everyone" was odd. It just felt like her awareness of her location as a being was "me watching me" — meaning, she felt like she was still the same person, but that she was looking at her physical body. She felt like she was still in her body; it didn't feel like she was not there. She experienced her conscious awareness as similar to when she was in her body. Leaving her body and being outside of her physical body felt the same as she felt now (during the interview), but looking down at her physical body. Being outside her physical body was not a memory that she had. She felt like, "Wow, that was something odd, (yet) it was just kind of a natural thing." This event just felt like, "Okay, this is what is happening now." She didn't have any kind of panicky feeling. It never seemed like "hanging up there" wasn't supposed to happen like that.

She remembered that floating feeling, watching over this doctor and seeing him work on her physical body from a whole different angle, and really not questioning this situation. "A whole different angle" was this way of looking down on her body from a corner of that room, up above those lights. Looking down on her body just didn't seem odd. It seemed okay.

While watching this doctor work on her body, she felt no fear, no pain, and no weirdness about her experience. Hanging up there felt "kind of like there was no gravity." Leaving her body was just, like, hanging up there, looking down, above those lights. But hanging up there wasn't anything that seemed unusual to her at that time. And it still didn't seem unusual.

She never felt like she wasn't totally her. She just felt like she was above herself; she still felt like she was the same soul. Being above her body felt no different from how she felt right now (during the interview). She always felt a complete awareness of herself, because as she was hanging up there, it was just her up there. It wasn't like, "Oh, I'm a spirit now." Hanging above her body was just the totality of her person as she is aware of herself. Hanging above her physical body wasn't like being a different person; it was just her—her normal or usual self. Hanging up there she did not feel she was a different entity or anything, just the same soul or personality. It was just, whatever she is, she was that up there, watching this doctor do everything from above.

Looking down on her body was odd, but it never seemed odd to her. She never had a nervous feeling in her stomach or thought anything like, "Wow, that was weird." Well, she thought that if she was above herself, watching herself, it would seem odd to her, because, "Why am I up here, if I'm down there?" But when it was happening, hanging above her body was just like a natural thing. It didn't seem strange in any way. Looking down on her body was just what it was, and she was comfortable with that understanding. She didn't feel like leaving her body needed to be explained or anything. At the time, she just accepted that she had left her body. Then afterwards, she felt the same thing;

leaving her body never felt odd to her. It was just fine. That's the way looking down on her body happened.

She never felt like she was dead, like she was having a near-death experience or "that light thing." Leaving her body wasn't like that to her. She never felt like she had died or anything. It just felt like she was watching what her doctor was doing. Even when she had been run over by the car, she had never felt like she was going to die. She just never had any feeling of being scared or like she was "going somewhere else" or anything like that. She had some serious, major trauma to her body, but she always felt like she was okay. She never felt like, "Oh my God, I'm going to die." She didn't have her life flash before her eyes. Just during that one procedure, she was definitely out of her body, watching that doctor work on her mouth. There wasn't any awareness of any kind of pain from what he was doing to her.

She didn't actually remember when she came back down into her body and didn't know if that was unusual. She didn't remember moving or coming back in so she was back with her physical body or anything like that. It was just over, and that was it. She didn't have any kind of reaction to being outside her physical body at that time or afterward. She had no pain. She didn't really experience what they were doing to her physical body. She just watched what they were doing to her. Then she was on medication because she had all those other injuries, but she didn't really remember coming back into her physical body at all.

If someone asks about her leaving her body, or if she talks about hanging up there, leaving her body, whether or not they believe she left her body doesn't matter to her, because, "I just know what I know, and I was not in my body. I was looking down on it at the time." If someone she knows says, "That seems weird. Do you think it was the medicine?" or asks any of those type of questions, it never really bothers her. If other people are asking questions or are doubting her, it never really bothers her because hanging up there is just a fact in her head. Hanging up there is not something that was drug induced, she said. She knows what she knows, and she knows what she felt, and she knew where she was when she was watching herself from above. When her parents came in that next day to visit with her, she told them that hanging up there has always been something that was just in her mind right from the beginning. Hanging up there has never been a question of, did leaving her body happen? Leaving her body did happen.

This next account of a transformative out-of-body experience comes from a sixty-eight-year-old, Caucasian female widow. She had a master's degree and no religious affiliation. At the time this incident occurred, she was twenty-eight, had suffered from depression most of her life, and was seriously contemplating taking her own life and the lives of her children. Afterward, however, she never again considered suicide. *Please note: this story contains details of a sexual assault.*

This occurrence unfolded while it was still daylight. This woman had wanted her husband to come with her to a laundromat, but he'd decided he was too busy. She walked into the laundromat, which was empty. Then shortly after, a young man came in. She thought, "Oh great! At least there is someone here in case somebody negative comes along. At least he'll be here to stop them." But as she was putting some clothes in the dryer, he came up behind her and grabbed her. He dragged her into the restroom and proceeded to rape her.

She remembered that as he was raping her, he put her down on the floor and said, "Do not scream or anything." But she went ahead and screamed anyway, hoping someone would hear and help her. So he started banging her head against that floor and knocked her unconscious. And when he did, she came out of her body. She just watched what was happening from overhead, with no emotion attached. She basically floated out of her body and observed from a different position than where her body was. She felt she was being separated and disconnected. She watched these events as a neutral observer. She was surprised that she wasn't emotionally attached to what was happening. She thought that detachment was her body protecting her from this trauma. She was just viewing an event at that time.

She saw the young man not only rape her, but also bite her body, draw blood, damage her body, and tear her clothes. He also tried to strangle her. When this young man was through, he just left, leaving her still unconscious.

When she was unconscious, she saw a bright light. At the beginning of this bright light was a tunnel. There was a dark figure there, and he said to her, "You can go ahead on through to the end of the tunnel if you choose."

She said, "What about my children? I want to bring them with me."

He said, "You can't do that. You either have to stay here or come with me, but you cannot bring your kids. It is really your decision right now."

At that time, she was going through a depression, and she had wanted to die. She had tried to figure out ways to commit suicide without imposing on or burdening anybody. She wanted to somehow bring her children with her because she felt her husband didn't know how to care for them properly. She thought her children would be safer with her. But when this dark figure told her that she couldn't bring her children, she decided to come back and finish her life on earth.

He explained to her that she had a choice: she could either go or stay, but it was her choice. She was in a depression, and she was very tempted to go. This dark figure also said, "You still have things to accomplish before you go, anyway. Otherwise, you'll just have to come back in another life and start all over again."

She thought she knew this dark figure dressed in black. She did recognize him at that time. However, during the interview, she couldn't tell me who that dark figure was. During the encounter with him, it felt as though she were being taken care of for the first time in years, since she was a baby.

The dark figure was somebody she was comfortable with, and she was very tempted to go. But she had still felt the tugging of her children to return to her life. It was very tempting, but she was not interested in starting over again. She said that if she had committed suicide, then this lifetime would have been kind of wiped out, because she hadn't learned the lessons she was supposed to before she died naturally. So she didn't want to come back and start all over again. The thing is, she said, she had already done the hard part. She just wanted to keep going to "get it over with." She chose to come back into her body, and that was when she regained consciousness.

After she came back to consciousness, she started to get up and leave. There was a woman in the laundromat, and this woman asked her if she was okay. She was in shock, and she said only, "Yeah." She went to her car, and she drove home.

When she got home, she came into the house through the garage. Her husband was out there working.

He said, "What happened?"

She was in shock, so she couldn't respond to him. She wanted to go and take a shower, which was the worst thing she could have done. But her husband called the paramedics, who came and brought her to a hospital. Some medical staff did tests and examined her. The young man had strangled her to the point that these medical people were shocked she was still alive. When a police officer interviewed her, he said it was the first time he had ever seen a strangulation in that condition, to that point, where the victim had survived. She couldn't talk for two days, was on an intravenous infusion, and couldn't swallow properly.

This event affected her middle son, because he had seen her come in and heard her husband yelling. This son thought her husband had done something to her, because seeing all the blood and stuff was traumatic for him.

Going back to the light at the end of the tunnel that she had seen, she remembered that it was very peaceful and tranquil. It had been very tempting to just keep on going and just say, "The heck with everything," and leave it behind. She had just felt very content, with no anxiety. She had felt just very comfortable and just complacent. She described feeling just very peaceful, just a lot of joy, and a lack of any negative feelings, thoughts, or images.

But she still had felt the tugging of her children. "Are they going to be okay?" she had asked the dark figure. She had made a difficult decision to come back to this life.

That was all she could remember—that and just a feeling that it was wonderful, peaceful, tranquil, and very inviting. *Tranquil* would be the perfect word for it—just an overwhelming joy, with all positive and no negative involved, no human emotion. She said it had just seemed like if she were in the light past the end of the tunnel, she would be learning spiritual lessons, but she just wouldn't have all the negative garbage she carried around on this planet.

Afterward, she sought out others who had had similar experiences, to help her relate to and understand what had happened to her. After the event, her husband began reading a book about out-of-body experiences, the light and tunnel, and the choice to stay or go. She didn't read it, but each night she'd have a dream. She would dream about a chapter he had just read. The chapters would say things like everybody was beautiful, nobody had any pain, nobody had handicaps, everybody was loving, there was no fighting, and everybody was just very in their loving spirit during experiences like those she'd had.

Her oldest son later had an experience similar to hers. When he was six years old, he was swimming at his friend's pool. He went down to the bottom of the pool to fetch a toy and didn't come back up. So his host went down and retrieved him. Afterward, her son said he hadn't wanted to come back because it was so beautiful. He talked about the same light she had seen. That had happened around the same time as her experience. So she figured that what she had experienced wasn't unusual, and such experiences do happen.

Like many other individuals, this woman sought others to validate that she was not the only person to have such an experience of going toward a light and speaking to an unknown being. What makes her situation special was how it transformed her mental health: before the event, she had wanted to die, but afterward, she had a desire to fully live and finish her life's path.

An extraordinary out-of-body experience allowed one thirty-nine-year-old single white male artist to experience the world in a way his physical senses had not allowed him to before, as well as expanding his sense of time and space. He had no religious affiliation but considered himself spiritual. He was "ninety percent deaf," and said, "It's always been a struggle for me to hear certain things." Yet when he floated above his body, "at that moment I could hear better than I ever had in my life. ... I could hear conversations of people going around the whole neighborhood." He described seeing the bigger picture:

I could hear conversations in the next house very clearly. I could hear things across town. I could hear all kinds of things. I remember as I was floating above, my hearing and my eyesight changed dramatically, like I was able to see through my house, through the walls, where everything was. I remember looking at the neighbor's house. I could see right through into their house. So I guess I gained a sense of sight in a way that I didn't have as an earthbound spirit in human form. I saw two people, the neighbors walking around in their house, doing regular stuff.

I could hear stuff that was going on locally in the neighborhood. I could hear people talking on the other side of the neighborhood. I could see them. I could hear stuff that was going on, on the other side of town. I remember overlooking the city as I was at that point, and I could hear different stuff going on.

This all took place in a split second or two. It just happened quickly.

From these stories, you can begin to see how the structure of events and cause-and-effect can change as the limitations of the physical world are shifted or transcended. Such events can make lasting impressions on those who have experienced them. These individuals often made statements such as, "I can still see those images. Those images are burned in my mind." And these images seem to be more vivid and real than everyday images and experiences.

Throughout history, many people have reported having dreams that revealed future events and happenings. People still report having such dreams, but today, these events are often underreported and highly scrutinized. For many, dreams revealing the future are simply facts; they see no need to validate these dreams, as the dreams present subjective truth.

Experiencing something before it happens typically alters an individual's sense of sequential time and frequently leads them to question their assumptions about how our world works. What they were taught to believe is suddenly in question. Was what they saw a random coincidence, or was it a meaningful perception by their unconscious or soul? Is this kind of foreknowledge really that unusual, or is it just a forgotten way of perceiving?

When someone's body is in one place and her consciousness perceives something happening somewhere else, providing her with information and knowledge she wouldn't possibly know unless she were there, no one other than that person can prove or disprove what happened. Our inner selves can travel to other places in time. Our consciousness can expand beyond its physical limitations and travel to other locations, where we can observe, interact with, or alter what is happening, depending on the situation.

Scientists have attempted to study these from-a-distance influences. In 1973, Dr. Stanley Krippner published a journal article describing how images displayed by several thousand people during a Grateful Dead concert were picked up on by a person forty-five miles away.[4] In 1893, Carl Sextus knew that a hypnotist could influence someone at a distance and sometimes communicate telepathically.[5]

If we can, in fact, travel out of our bodies and, with a genuine good intention, positively alter another's life, then we would benefit from guarding our thoughts and from projecting positive outcomes. Is it also possible to negatively affect someone from a distance? And if it is, would that mean we need to protect ourselves from influences that attempt to take us to unhealthy places or down harmful paths? Why would we fear such phenomena when these negative and positive possibilities have already been recorded throughout history? And why would we think it is not possible for each of us to experience such phenomena when so many people without special abilities have already done so?

The woman who watched doctors tend to her body after she had been hit by a car also reported seeing through the ceiling and overhead lights of her hospital room, as if they were not there. Others who have traveled out of their bodies have talked about seeing through houses or walls and hearing others in their minds from an unusual distance. They all perceived things that an outside observer could not perceive with their five physical senses. These experiences raise the question of whether our souls have a perceptual awareness that is quite a bit more powerful than our normal, everyday physical bodies' abilities to take information from our surroundings. If our souls do indeed have this expanded awareness, it could explain how someone might see an event as if it had already happened. (I did an independent study with Dr. Don Rice at the University of West Georgia on precognitive research and cases. It was by far one of the most interesting research projects I participated in.) However, reaching out to our greater consciousness is not an easy task.

The cases described in this chapter are not everyday occurrences but happen nonetheless. We cannot say there are no red-haired women simply because children have been born without red hair. Similarly, a critic cannot dismiss knowledge and events simply because these experiences do not occur frequently or on demand.

Having an experience that defies the known workings of time and space can transform someone's life, and they may live quite differently, in a healthier, more positive way than before. These subjective changes are all that's needed to confirm that the occurrence was powerful and meaningful to the person who experienced it. No further external validation is needed.

Having talked with hundreds of people about their supernatural experiences, I have seen commonalities between the experiences that the individuals were not aware of. I also know that such events have been reported for hundreds of years. There is no finer scientific tool than the human being.

Reflections: Padre Pio, an Italian priest, stigmatic, and mystic, said that a person could pray for the peaceful death of a great-grandparent.[6] Time and space can be altered either separately or in combination. This altering of time and space can bring about a different type of connection between two related things in the present.

Acknowledging diverse perceptual possibilities may allow you to perceive and engage in connections that you had previously been taught were not possible, such as time traveling, entering an expanded space, or interacting with or altering events from a distance.

Breaking free of your old beliefs, which are based on your past experience, allows you to experience new ways of perceiving as you travel through uncharted territory. Sometimes when you experience something different with your body, you realize there are new potentials within yourself. I remember doing reverse curls with 100-pound weights at the gym; I would routinely do three sets of fifteen repetitions. One day I felt like I had lost strength, as the sets seemed unusually difficult to do. When I finished and was taking the weights off, I realized I had been curling 110 pounds. My body had been ready to move forward even though my mind had not been consciously prepared to do so.

What potentials are waiting for you to realize their availability within you?

Exercises: Spend some time on each of the following perception-expanding exercises:

1. Make a list of things you wouldn't normally think or imagine could be connected. For example, you might imagine a fawn and a mountain lion cub huddled together during a forest fire, a leafy green tree covered in snow in November, or two enemies coming together to take on a mutual threat.

2. How many different ways in time and space can you understand a statement from a loved one? For example, can something you say or do in the present alter the past or change the future in some way?

3. Make a list of things you would like to change in your life. How you can see each of them in different time and space perspectives. For example, if you could communicate with someone internally at a distance or someone who is no longer on the earth, how would that ability change how you interact with others?

Chapter 5

Perceiving through Feelings and Thoughts

We are often not aware of alternative ways of perceiving our environment and our universe until a supernatural experience shows us these ways. To perceive something in a new, unfamiliar way can be exhilarating and scary. Perceiving beings or events via unexpected thoughts or feelings, rather than seeing them with our physical eyes, is an interesting form of supernatural awareness. Afterward, you may struggle to justify your extraordinary means of perception and what it showed you, which you have come to regard as a fact.

For example, a biracial male doctoral student in his thirties, who said he was spiritual but not religious, described lying down on his bed after meditating. He was getting ready to go to sleep for the night. Suddenly he had a feeling a woman had walked right through the door to his apartment. She was wearing jeans and a black leather coat. However, he only felt and thought this woman was there; he didn't see her as an external visual or even as an internal image. He couldn't explain how he knew what she was wearing or why that thought had entered his awareness. He felt the knowledge as an external influence intruding upon his stream of consciousness. The thought appeared foreign against his natural flow of thoughts.

He felt her come directly into his bedroom and lie down on his bed. He felt all the sensations of someone lying in his bed, including the weight of her body leaving an impression on it. This event disturbed him so much he got out of bed and went outside on his porch, just to change the situation.

How did this new way of perceiving enter his consciousness when he had never even imagined such a possibility before?

Can you perceive something as green without seeing that color? Can you know something is sharp without seeing or touching that object? If so, how do you come to such knowledge and awareness? To feel your way through an experience is sometimes the only way, though the feelings may defy the logic of your past learnings. Focusing on this way of perceiving through feelings can enhance your ability to do it.

This next case was presented by a forty-eight-year-old, Caucasian, divorced mother of three, of Mormon faith, who worked in sales. She had become quite comfortable with her ability to distinguish information she'd come to perceive through her feelings. Earlier in her life, as a Mormon missionary, she would go out and talk to people about spiritual experiences, about Jesus, and about her church. One day she had come home, walked into her apartment, and could just feel her (deceased) great-uncle and great-aunt standing there.

This woman described what experiencing their presence was like: Usually when she walks into a familiar place and sees someone, she recognizes who the person is. When she walked into her apartment, she had that same feeling of recognition but without actually seeing anyone, either in the apartment or in her mind's eye. She couldn't see those relatives but felt their presence just as if she were sitting in the same room with anyone else. She just knew who was there, and she could just feel their presences because of the relationship she'd had with these relatives and the way she had felt when she'd been with them in the past. She didn't really hear anything. She just felt like it all happened to her mind. It was as if she had just walked into the room, and someone said, "What are you doing here?" It felt like finding an individual sitting in your house when you didn't expect them to be there. That is how these presences felt—like these relatives had walked in and were standing there, waiting for her, without any inner or outer visual presentation.

She had communicated with her great-aunt and -uncle through thought. She could communicate in her mind, without words or anything. She could feel a conversation, just as she could just feel their presence there. She asked these relatives, using her mind, "What are you doing here?" They told her that they were being missionaries, like she was at the time. But they were teaching "this lady's mother" — meaning the mother of a woman she had recently been speaking to in her work as a missionary — on the other side.

In our interview, she said her spirit was communicating with their spirits. She received a response back in words, but this response was not like the words she and I were speaking out loud and hearing there in my office. She got just thoughts or words in her mind.

And then she experienced a visual image about what these relatives were telling her. They said they were there teaching or working with "this lady's mother," and then she saw them with the mother of the lady in question as this picture in her mind. And she said, "Oh, okay."

The next day she was with the lady in question in person, teaching her and her family. She and this lady were actually having a discussion, and in the middle of that discussion, she could feel her great-aunt and -uncle and this lady's mother walk into this room. And when they did, she and this lady looked up at that exact same space. She described it "as if you were talking to someone and all of a sudden, like, a guest appeared. You would stop and acknowledge this guest." These relatives walked in, and she stopped talking. She and this lady both kind of stopped and looked at the door. Then they kind of glanced at each other and just went back to talking. But the presences entering the room definitely broke up what she and this lady were doing.

These relatives wanted to show the lady's mother that their niece was there, teaching her daughter exactly the same thing that these relatives were teaching her on the other side. After that, the lady's mother looked at her. Then she looked at her daughter.

This woman said it felt like the lady she was talking to had felt the same thing she had. She didn't know for sure because they did not discuss what happened. And honestly, feeling such presences was just a fact—it just happened—and then after that she didn't ever feel them around her again.

In her story, this former Mormon missionary demonstrated the internal process of making sense of unusual perceptual experiences. This next story further illustrates this process. The individual who shared it was a fifty-five-year-old mother of Scandinavian, English, and Irish descent and Methodist faith. She seemed to "know" things she really had no way of knowing through "normal channels." Instead, she said, she "feels them."

By "feels," she meant that, in this particular incident, she felt goosebumps and chills everywhere, as if she were feverish, but she wasn't. It was as if those goosebumps on her body were somehow being continually stimulated, and they were running over her body like waves continually crashing on the shore. It was really hard for her to explain the experience differently. By "normal channels," she meant that these transmissions of information or energy she received were not the type of communication one routinely thinks of or experiences. These communications didn't come through a phone, e-mails, text messages, or other means that are considered "normal." These messages came, in her case, as bodily sensations of goosebumps.

She and her aunt had taken a long road trip from Seattle to Los Angeles to see how her mother was doing. This woman had lost her maternal grandmother a few months earlier, on her mother's birthday.

They had been driving all day, and when they arrived at her mother's home, she felt a need for a nice hot cup of coffee. So while her mother and aunt chatted at the table, she started making coffee. She was standing at that stove with her back to them. As she started to put some sweetener in her coffee, waves of chills overtook her entire body, from head to toe, and radiated around her, over and over. These chills almost made it difficult for her to stand for a moment. It sort of felt like her knees were going to give out.

For a second she felt "zoned out." She couldn't really explain this zoned-out part. She was "lost in that moment." She didn't really know how to explain it, other than to say that nothing else but that moment mattered. That moment had her full attention!

From behind her, her mother gasped and said, "Barbara, you have twinkling lights all over you!" She turned around to face her mother and aunt.

"Gigi!" She and her mother both said it at the same time.

Gigi was her recently deceased grandmother, and she and her mother had both known that her grandmother had just come to hug her. She has been "hugged" this way many times over the years, but this experience in her mother's kitchen was her most powerful episode and strongest sensation by far. Looking at her mother, she *knew* they were in tune with each other. After all, they had both said "Gigi" at that same time. And they knew, somehow, instinctively, what each other was thinking—like their thoughts were connected!

What she had felt as her chills, and what her mother had seen as lights, somehow told them both who it was. It was as if Gigi told each of them that this was her, even though they didn't hear her say such words. Without question, they just knew. This thought was with them both. It was her mother who called the experience "getting a big hug" from her grandmother. She had been her, Gigi's, first grandchild, and the bond between them, that deep love, was powerful.

This woman said she had physically felt things like these chills or these sensations of goosebumps on other occasions. She hadn't known her maternal grandfather, as he and Gigi had divorced when her mother was four years old. She had gone to Salt Lake City to meet his wife, her step-grandmother, about three months after her grandfather had died. She had known nothing about him, but she had wanted to learn about him. So she had traveled to Salt Lake City with her aunt. His widow had invited them to stay that night, and she had slept in her grandfather's bedroom, in his bed. She was almost asleep when she felt someone get into bed with her. She couldn't figure out why her aunt or her step-grandmother would be climbing into the bed. She turned over to see if this person, whoever it was, was okay. She was alone. Nevertheless, she sensed someone "crawling" into the bed and the movements of the bed in response. She felt the tug of the covers. Still, she was alone, as no one she could see was there. She felt every movement that one feels it when someone is getting into bed next to them: the weight of someone lying down on that other side of the bed, pulling her a little to that side, and the covers moving as the bed was pressed down from the weight of this person. It felt as if a person were getting into bed with her.

In our interview, she said she hoped she was not wasting my time because she was not sure her story was what I was looking for. She said she knew that others could hear and could talk with people "on the other side of the veil" (meaning, where we cross over from this life to the other side).

She had a degree of fear of spirits. She didn't want to be startled by a sudden presence. Her mother had told her that none of their loved ones who had gone before would want to scare her, so they hugged her to let her know of their presence. She had had a couple "strong sensory visits," as she called them, but not a lot. She had had more than one episode of this nature, where the sense of touch and her body's reaction to what was happening was strong.

This woman's experiences reminded me of something I experienced as a child. At that age, I sometimes saw movies depicting romances between a Native American female tribal leader and a male European captain or leader of some group of Caucasian people, and I would get goosebumps and feel waves of energy rushing down my arms, legs, and back. Later, when I was a teenager, my paternal grandmother told me that there had been a Native American "princess" in our family. My great-9-grandfather was Chief Madockawando, a grand *sachem* of the Abenaki nation in the 1600s. His daughter, my great-8-grandmother, married a French baron named Vincent de Saint-Castin, my great-8-grandfather. Their lives demonstrated immense responsibility, many traumas, and great pain and suffering. Years later, when I was an adult, I found documents validating the story my grandmother had told me.

This way of knowing through bodily sensations can have a dark side. Sometimes things happen that can make us uncertain of the boundaries and dimensions of our personal world and our universe. This next case is a frightening example.

The woman who shared it with me was a thirty-six-year-old Caucasian housewife with a bachelor's degree in communications. She was of Catholic faith. She said she had had many nighttime experiences where she woke up and was paralyzed, unable to move, and felt a being, something very strong, force itself on top of her in an overpowering way. It just moved on top of her, she said. She described it as something very evil, demon like. Yet it also had arms and legs and was humanlike—just like a big guy, with long hair. It would hold her down on her sides, on her hands, and on her ribs.

Perhaps there had been more than one being. She hadn't seen them; she'd *felt* them. It literally had felt like they were on top of her, doing something. She really hadn't known what was going on or what they were doing. She had been jerked out of her bed, and they had grabbed at her side, above her hip, with really long fingers. Many times she had felt hands come underneath her blankets and just grab at her arms or legs or whatever they could hold on to. This being or beings would just jerk her and take her right out of her bed. She didn't see anything; she just felt it. In the morning, when she woke up, she remembered only that something had lain on top of her.

One particularly memorable version of these experiences had happened six or seven years prior to our interview. She remembered waking early in the morning and feeling this force pulling her "back under," or back to sleep. Her alarm clock had gone off, and she had tried to get up. Yet this being had pulled her "back under," to a sleep state where she was both asleep and awake. She had tried several times to shake her head and come out of her sleeping, but the force kept pulling her back down. She had felt as if she were awake, yet at the same time she wasn't. It kept pulling her back under even though she kept trying to wake up. She wasn't even sleeping.

The next thing she felt was "this heavy force," this massive being, whatever it was, on top of her. She couldn't really recall a feeling of having sex with somebody. Yet she remembered having this feeling that maybe what this being was trying to do was have sex with her. He was just very forceful and very brutal. She really almost had that feeling that this was truly what was going on.

This being was just massive and huge. He was not alien like, but more demon like. He was on top of her and was holding her sides so tight that it was painful that she almost couldn't breathe. Then she actually couldn't breathe. This being wouldn't let her go anywhere. She tried so hard to shake herself out of her sleep. But he would just pull her back down and hold her sides. His fingers grabbing her sides, her ribs, and just digging in, were painful. He squeezed so tight that it cut off her breathing.

She discerned that he had long hair. She could feel his long hair on her arms. She tried grabbing his long hair several times. She tried everything to try to get him off her, but there was nothing she could do. She could just feel his arms, his legs, his whole body—everything was massive, big, and huge.

She remembered fighting so hard. She had thought she was going to die as she felt this power of whatever this being was. She thought he was trying to kill her because he was cutting off her breath. He was just so heavy on top of her. She couldn't fight back. She had nothing against him and felt powerless.

A few years later, she had become engaged to a man. One night she had a dream, and in that dream, she saw an image of that same demon-like being who had come to her in her sleep. It was what she pictured that being looking like from a distance. This being told her that if she didn't leave her fiancé, he (the being) was going to "take care of him." Her fiancé was going to get in the way, the being said. He didn't like this fiancé and didn't want him around. He was going get rid of him.

She was so scared! What is she going to do? She knew that these experiences with the being had been going on, off and on, for some time. She had been having this kind of experience of someone grabbing her at night.

The morning after the dream, she told her fiancé about what she had dreamt. Her fiancé told her, "You know me. I read the Bible. I don't have bad dreams. But last night I had a bad dream. I felt the presence of something evil in the room. ... I swear— and you know this much—that dream was really weird." For her fiancé to say he had felt the same thing—that was weird, because, as he said, he didn't usually have bad dreams. Before that night, she said, he could never have even related to anything that she might have told him. She is married to him now. At the time of the interview, she reported having had no further incidents with the being.

The idea of taking in information via unexpected emotional sensations, physical sensations unrelated to our physical environment, or sudden, seemingly random thoughts may seem strange at first. We're so used to perceiving the world through just our eyes. This change in perception is akin to a movie in which warriors close their eyes or lose their sight, but then hone other ways of knowing in order to fight well and defend themselves. Or you could compare this change to when you are sick or injured, and suddenly the sensations from a part of your body that usually operates automatically, without your awareness, are all you notice.

Many individuals have described to me very similar experiences of perceiving something unseen. A twenty-six-year-old, married Caucasian female shared this example:

I felt pressure on my chest and abdomen, but (it) felt like my arms and legs were being pinned. I struggled to get out of bed but couldn't do it. There were small bruises on the tops of my arms. At first, it was just the sensation of someone being on top of me. Then I had pains in my arms and legs, like someone digging in their fingers and kneeling on me. Random pains all over followed that. The more I struggled the worse it felt. I stopped struggling, and it subsided after what seemed like a few minutes.

A twenty-nine-year-old married, Catholic, Caucasian nurse, with a bachelor's degree in nursing, described an experience in which she felt her body had been violated by an invisible presence in her bed at night. She felt, heard, and smelled this presence. Here is a portion of her account:

I crawled back into bed and was almost asleep, like when you can feel yourself drifting and then going deeper and deeper, and somehow in your mind, you know you are about to sleep. I was somewhere in that realm, when just as I lay there in my own house—a house I have had for six years—I got lost. I tried to wake up, making my eyes open, and they wouldn't. I had a fear.

I felt something at the same time. There was this odor— really strong, really repulsive, worse than dirty garbage. Nothing I ever smelled before. If I had to put (it into) a word, I would say *burnt oil*, or like antifreeze that was bad or burnt, or like something dead laying in the road, all combined in one smell. I can still smell it.

I felt something on me, on my thighs, working its way up like a closed hand—more like hard and with a lot of pressure. … Something forceful, not like a loving hand, caressing me. Like someone grabbing their way to me. … I looked so hard to see what it was, and there was *nothing* there. (Afterward there were) bruises… blue and black and stretched out, not round in any way, more like streaks, mostly on my inner thighs.

A more positive experience of feeling and knowing without visual or verbal interaction was well described by a retired thirty-one-year-old police officer. She was of German, Irish, and Native American background and had a master's degree. She told me about an interaction she'd had with an ex-boyfriend who had passed away:

I felt him sit down next to me, and if I was to close my eyes, I could have felt him. … I would just feel my ex-boyfriend walk into a room, and I didn't understand it. Just very similar, like, I would say, if you were taking a nap on a couch and you were in a light sleep and I walked in the room and you just kind of stirred a little bit and you knew I was there. It felt like that sensation…

I would be cooking or cleaning, and all of the sudden… (it) felt like the air would change… or I would feel it pass by.

I would feel somebody walk into the room... (When it's) somebody you know really well, like your brother, your sister, your dad, you know what it feels like when they walk into a room, when their energy is present. And that is what it felt like.

I would have to stop and turn around, and he obviously wasn't there because he passed away. But I didn't know he had passed away at that time.

It got to the point where it would happen pretty frequently. I would say out loud, "Not today. Leave me alone. You know I don't want to deal with it." And I'd ask him to stop, and he would. That sounds weird because he had passed, but he would.

We did have a conversation without words. I don't know how to elaborate. ... If there was such thing as telepathy, where I could sit here and make my thoughts known to you, I think that would be the equivalent. It was just like a conveyance of knowledge. There were no words, but I knew what he was saying, like when you slow dance with someone you love.

Another example of this type of phenomenon was described by a fifty-four-year-old male artist. He said that as he was lying in bed, his exposed flesh felt tingly and caused him to rub his face and neck. He heard swallowing noises that were really weird, and his hair began standing up on the back of his head. He heard two footsteps on either side of his pillow; he heard the footsteps go crunch, crunch and felt his pillow move. He saw nothing visually, but he felt and heard sensations. He then sensed more than two footsteps. He estimated that this experience lasted forty-five seconds to a minute, but it seemed like a lot longer to him at the time. (Like this man, other people who have had similar experiences also report having a sense of expanded time.)

Yet another report came from a thirty-five-year-old Caucasian man, who was a director in information technology. He recounted an incident that happened when he was seven years old. He perceived his bedcovers "pressing up against my leg and feeling the pressure of someone sitting on the edge of my bed." He knew it was a middle-aged woman, even though he did not see her visually. He felt the pressure of a hand pressing the covers down on the opposite side of him from no known source. He ended up fleeing to his grandparents' room. At the end of our interview, he said of the incident, "It's always been ingrained in my mind and pressed in my memory, like it happened yesterday."

In these incidents, the person experiencing them *felt* what was happening with their emotions and their physical body, but they *saw* nothing. The only visible evidence of the encounter were the indentations on the bed or bruises on the body after the fact. Sometimes people report smelling scents or hearing sounds that have no logically identifiable point of origin. I remember one individual telling me he had heard something breathing by the side of his bed, but could not see or otherwise identify the source.

These experiences suggest that there are invisible forces and influences moving around us. These moments of supernatural awareness can open us to perceiving more of our universe. And without such firsthand experiences, our supernatural abilities might otherwise remain dormant.

Do goosebumps and chills tell you things too? Are you accustomed to interpreting or receiving these sensations as genuine means of perceiving information? Do you need some sort of external confirmation before you believe that the knowledge brought to you by such feelings or by unexpected thoughts is real or true? Why are external validations so much more important and emphasized in modern times than this internal way of validating information? Is your power of perception being expanded by those who insist that everything you know must come to you through your external senses, or is it stripped away from you by experts who want to determine what you think and feel and why? Have your body and emotions, which are instruments of understanding, been dulled and weakened?

If you would like to awaken new ways of perceiving, consider the stories shared in this chapter. Seeing how others make sense of how they perceived beings and events through something other than sight can help you open to more diverse perceptions and to unseen aspects of our universe.

Reflections: Remember, other ways of perceiving can help you find new ways of connecting with our complex universe. Encouraging yourself to find new ways of perceiving may allow you to engage differently with things and ideas.

Past learnings may have given you a bias that says there's only one way of perceiving or receiving information about beings, things, and events. Letting go of this bias and embracing the idea that there might be other ways of perceiving can open you to new experiences and connections with your world. For example, a mentor once taught me that hypnosis is not a way for someone else to take control of your mind, but a tool that teaches you how to control your own mind. When I thought about hypnosis this way, I realized that in order to gain awareness, I had to let go and really hear what was being said. When I was able to do that, I could respond accurately rather than automatically acting as if I knew more than I did. (Sometimes during hypnosis, people don't even hear an instruction. Instead, they just act in a routine manner — that is, with meaning they project inaccurately onto the situation.)

Here's another example: A friend of mine related an instance when she entered a business meeting in a conference room. "That's funny," she said to the others in the room. "I was really relaxed, and now I feel angry." A couple of people in the room told her there had been a heated argument in that room just a few minutes prior to her arrival. Although she had not perceived a change in emotional atmosphere, others helped her make this connection by pointing out circumstances happening before her arrival and how she perceived something that was not visible at the moment.

There are those who wish to manipulate and dominate others and those who wish to empower others. To manipulate or dominate is to replace freedom with false limitations and distorted perceptions that keep you where you are. To empower is to release you from false limitations. To empower is to give you the ability to see accurately. The question is, are those who try to convince us there is only one way of perceiving trying to manipulate and dominate us, or are they trying to empower us?

Exercises: Work through each of these three exercises slowly:

1. In a given situation or for a specific amount of time, try not to think or see what is happening but instead feel what is going on around you. For example, you are lying on a bed with your eyes closed and sense that someone is in your room. You open your eyes and can't see any being in the room. You close your eyes again. Can you feel them? Can you hear them? What tells you they are there? What makes it feel like someone is in the room with you? What about the room feels different from how you usually experience it? Maybe you can hear breathing or smell a scent associated with that person, such as cologne. What other details can you identify?

2. Try to notice when your moods and emotions change suddenly or unexpectedly. Identify what is causing these changes or what is different in your circumstances around that time. Can you identify a logical reason for a change? If so, then the change was not prompted by something supernatural. But if you sense a change may be triggered or influenced by something you can't quite comprehend, consider the possibility your supernatural awareness is expanding to take in new, extraordinary or extrasensory information.

3. Try to feel your way through a day. At the end of the day, journal about what has taken place and how you perceived it. Did you experience any unexpected or unusual changes in how or what you were feeling? Looking back, do you think there is a possibility your feelings were affected by something that was not perceivable by your usual senses?

Part II

Interacting with Other Beings

The cases in Part II demonstrate interactions with extraordinary entities and objects and the major changes that can occur in us as a result. Acknowledging influences you had never suspected existed can expand your perceptual possibilities and potential, expose you to the possibility that death is not the end for your loved ones or yourself, and enable you to understand our universe in a whole new way.

Chapter 6

Interaction with External Influences: Creatures

When most people think of interacting with external influences, stories of angels, demons, and other nonearthly creatures inevitably come up. These kinds of cases suggest that our universe is inhabited not just by beings and creatures we can see, but by a variety of invisible beings too.

A twenty-eight-year-old divorced mother of Baptist faith, with some college education, experienced a vision of a demon and angels. It was her first and most awkward supernatural experience, and she was thirteen at the time. She was spending the night at her grandmother's house and awakened at around 3 a.m. while sleeping next to her grandmother. She had a vision of her cousin Carole. In the vision, she saw through Carole's ceiling into her bedroom. She said it was as if there were a light showing her what was going on in the room. She wasn't actually *in* the room, though. She could see but could not smell, hear, taste, or touch. Both Carole and her bed were in view, and they were colorless. There seemed to be no noise.

Carole was sleeping and didn't seem to notice anything. She looked peaceful. She was lying on a tall bed. Above her was a small, powerful demon, with two angels on either side of it, using all of their might to pull this evil entity away from her cousin.

The girl saw the colors of these angels and the demon but not so much the rest of the picture. The rest of the room wasn't visible, perhaps because she was only supposed to see what was going on in the "fight," she guessed.

The demon was as small as a toddler—maybe no more than two feet tall. The best way she could describe his figure was to say it was like the green demon in the (1997 animated) Disney movie *Hercules*. This demon's head looked like it had two points protruding out of it. This demon's color wasn't gray, but it wasn't brown either. His color seemed more like that of dead flesh, as if she were looking at a dead man who was moving. The two protruding points on his head were more like extended skin than horns. They were shaped like horns, but their color and texture were identical to that of his flesh. These horns began at his head and went straight to sharp points at the tips.

She felt so much evil from this demon because of the way he was trying to get at her cousin. The feeling she felt was similar to what she assumed an abuser or bad person would make someone feel. The room seemed to have a thick tension in it. It seemed like at any minute this thing could snap, and her cousin could get harmed or even die. This demon was being held back, and it was as if the angels were protecting her cousin from him.

This demon's motion looked like a fire when it shoots embers or, as the woman put it, like "spit fire." She watched him spark as a fire sparks. While he was being held back, he "sparked" to try and get away. He was harshly trying to release himself from the angels with his physical movement. It was easy to see this demon's mission was to harm Carole. He was relentless and powerful. He had an energy that would scare anyone enough to eventually want to just pray for safety.

Again, there were two angels, one on either side of this evil entity. It looked as if they were using all of their might to pull at the demon while he was trying to go after her cousin. They were grasping him in an arm lock, locking his elbows at the sides. It seemed like these angels were really working, considering there were two of them.

She knew this was a serious fight between the angels and the demon because of the thick tension in the room. These angels were teaming up together and fighting to keep this evil entity away from her cousin Carole as she slept. In a split second, the fight could have gone either way, though it also felt like good would win regardless. She felt this demon could snap because he was mad about being held back. In any given moment, if he had the chance to harm her cousin, he would. She could feel that evil coming off him. This demon was only out to harm. There was no good from him at all.

The angels were magnificent! She thought they were probably over seven feet tall, though their long gowns could have added length. Their gowns were white with a pale gold. They had white wings that began with a round top over their heads and ended at points around the ends of the gowns. (In our interview, she noted that now, as an adult, she collected angel figures and was "very picky on the wings" because of this vision experience.) She did not know if their wings were feathery or what. Her main focus was on how these angels were pulling at this demon.

She was not scared this demon would harm her, but she was afraid for her cousin. This entire vision happened in a matter of seconds. And after just a few seconds of it, enough for her to get what was going on, she woke right up. This demon wasn't giving up, and his strength had scared her to the point that she woke.

She looked at the clock (which said 3:00 a.m.). She quickly shook her grandmother and said, "Wake up, Grandma! There's something bad after Carole." Her grandma didn't have time to question anything because as soon as she had spoken, the phone began to ring.

It was Carole. "Aunt Mildred, something bad is after me!" she said.

Her grandma then began praying loudly in tongues and continued praying for about a half hour or so. The girl didn't pray with her grandmother; she had no clue what her grandmother was saying. She also didn't know how long her grandmother prayed. At that point, she was no longer looking at the time.

After a while, Carole told her grandma that she felt better, and they all went back to bed.

This situation was not something that happens every day, the woman said. But for her, every bit of this experience was as real as could be. She didn't understand how she could see what she did like she did, but she did see it. The phone call from her cousin to her grandmother had validated it. She did wonder why this particular thing had never happened to her again.

Is it possible for external influences to affect someone who alters their consciousness with substances? Or could external influences even be the reason behind someone's substance abuse? These are questions this next case may bring to mind. The woman who experienced it was a forty-one-year-old married mother and phlebotomist. She was Brazilian and of the Catholic faith. English was her second language.

She had gone to visit her friend, Rae, and say goodbye to her, because Rae was moving to Atlanta. Rae was at the house of another friend, Kate. When the woman arrived at Kate's house, Rae and Kate invited her to have supper.

The woman was sitting in Kate's living room while Kate was in the kitchen, cooking. The woman started having a headache. It was not like a normal headache. It felt like someone was pushing her with both hands, and her head was being smushed or crushed. The pressure felt just heavy. It was like something was pushing on her forehead specifically. And she had "sprinkles," or a ticklish feeling, on her forehead and scalp. It felt like a person was tapping on her forehead with their fingers. (In our interview, she demonstrated what she felt by tapping all over her own forehead with her fingertips.) This pushing sensation and heaviness were on her forehead only. This pushing or this pressure felt like someone was pushing her, like "when you knead bread, you press with repeated pressure to make it smashed," she said. For her, these feelings were physical, yet they also were not physical.

She felt "out of this space" when she had this headache. It was like she couldn't control her headache. Internally, she had a lot of voices, talking, and visions, but it was all blurry. She didn't see anything; it was just dark—meaning she could see, but the images were dark. She could only visualize inside what she was being told.

As she was sitting there, Kate said to her, "Oh, come over and try my food." Then she, Rae, and Kate went and sat at

Kate's kitchen table. All of a sudden, as Kate served her, she saw shadows behind Kate. Two, three—she didn't know how many. These shadows were all laughing—sarcastically, not happily. And then they said, "You cannot do nothing with her. She is ours. She belongs to us."

The woman was looking at these shadows. She could hear them. She didn't see their faces. She perceived them as probably a male, a female—two at least, maybe three. Meanwhile, her headache started getting stronger and stronger as she was sitting there.

As she was about to eat, she said to her friends, "I have to leave. I'm sorry, but I have to leave."

Kate said, "Oh, maybe she doesn't like my food."

"No, it's not your food. Your food is good," the woman said. "I really have to leave. I'm not feeling good."

"Okay," Kate said.

The woman said bye to her friends and left.

The next day she called her friend Rae to apologize for leaving so quickly. She said, "I want to tell you when I was in your friend's (Kate's) house, I had this big headache, and I saw shadows behind your friend."

"Shadows?" Rae said.

"Yeah, and they weren't nice. They were bad. And then they said, 'You cannot do nothing with her. She's ours. She belongs to us.'"

"Really?" Rae said. "Is that because she is drinking?"

"Does she drink?" the woman asked.

"Yeah, she drinks really heavily," Rae said.

"Oh, okay," the woman replied. She and Rae talked a little more, and then she hung up the telephone. Rae then called Kate to tell her what she had said.

"Oh, what are you talking about?" Kate replied.

Later on that week, Kate got arrested. Her family had to go and bail her out of jail.

The next day, a neighbor of Kate's invited Kate to go to a church. Kate went, and when the service was done, this minister's wife asked Kate to go and meet with her husband.

This minster said, "I have to talk to you about something."

"What?" she said.

"You know you have a demon possession behind you," he told her.

She said, "What are you talking about?"

"We are going to pray for you," he said. "But you have to pray for you too. You have to help you. If you're not willing to help you, we cannot help you. But we are going to pray for you." Kate thought the minister had seen this shadow (behind her) because this shadow was so strong. He said to Kate, "You have to take care of yourself. Go home." He also gave Kate some verses of the Bible to read.

Kate went home and made a phone call to her friend Rae, who by that time had moved to Atlanta. She said to Rae, "You know what you told me about what your friend said yesterday? Your friend was right, because I went to the church and even this pastor said I have bad demons. So now what is this? She said I had shadows. This pastor said I had demons."

And Rae said to Kate, "See, it might be a sign. You have to take care of yourself and your addiction. ... You know what you have to do."

So the next day, Kate went to a rehabilitation center and tried to fix her addiction.

Rae called the woman I interviewed to tell her what had happened with Kate. Finding out about these events validated her earlier internal vision experience. Rae said, "I thank you. I thank you for her. What you said helped her like a wake-up call."

Some interactions with external forces can make us question the boundaries of our being. This next individual had a uniquely mental and physical interaction with an external influence. He was a fifty-five-year-old divorced father, of Catholic faith and French-Canadian, Irish, and Native American descent.

He was sitting in his recliner, half awake. He would snooze for a bit and then wake up. When he felt cold on his left side, at first he thought he might be having a daydream. Then he felt a hand touch his left shoulder. This hand was ice cold. He felt its icy touch slide across his shoulder, down his short-sleeved shirt, and down to the skin of his bicep to his elbow. This touch was soft, and its pressure against his shoulder was soft. This touch felt as though he had put an ice gel pack on his shoulder. The entire room became very cold too.

He went "into a daze." Or perhaps it was better to say that it startled him. He hadn't been expecting this to happen. This occurrence was a shock but didn't wake him. Again, it seemed like he was having a daydream.

Then he could see himself from above, which he found odd. It was like being in a loft and seeing himself below. A voice called out his name. This voice speaking to him was female, and it was talking with a soft, sensual whispering. He had never heard this voice before. It was like the woman speaking was behind his chair, leaning over the chair, looking at him. She wasn't there to hurt him or bother him. She seemed familiar, as if this was not their first encounter. But he had no memory of any other encounter with her.

Back in the chair, he opened his eyes, and he was shaking. He was so cold, and he wasn't sure what had just happened. He was scared. It was the most scared he has ever been. He felt he had been touched by something. He couldn't identify or explain this experience and feared he sounded crazy.

He walked around his apartment to see if anyone was there. Although the temperature was warm outside, in the mid-eighties, he closed all the windows and felt like he should turn on the heat in the apartment. But he didn't. This experience scared him so much that he shook for an hour. He ended up leaving his apartment and going for a walk. When he came back, his apartment was too warm. He opened his windows to cool his apartment down.

The feeling of cold in this man's story is akin to another encounter shared by a thirty-five-year-old, married, Caucasian female, of no religious faith. She reported a freezing cold feeling during her encounter with an extraordinary entity:

> When I sat up on the edge of the couch, one of the beams of light took more of a defined shape of a human form and came towards me. And as it came towards me, this form became darker.
>
> As soon as it reached me, I felt it. My whole body got extremely cold—freezing cold. It appeared to go through me because when it reached me and my body turned cold, I lost my breath. It was almost like you were going down a rollercoaster, how you have that dip and your belly kind of comes up into your throat. It was that kind of a feeling.

Instead of feeling cold, the man in the next case felt warmth. He was a forty-five-year-old, unemployed, single white male with a high school education. He was in the hospital and had had surgery to remove his appendix. He said the stitches from the surgery hadn't held, and the doctor and nurses had "stitched him up again" without pain medicine. As the medical personnel left his room, he was distraught, crying, and felt like dying. He described what happened next:

> There was a spark of light (that came) into my room, on the right-hand corner of this room. Then this spark of light went off. I could only feel this spark moving in the air and start to light up again as I noticed this spark now on my left-hand side of this room.

Then this spark moves again. This spark came to the middle of this room. This spark of light came on again, and my whole inside just lit right up. Then this spark came closer and closer, with a giant heap of light behind this spark, one big flash of light, only this spark was a flood of light. My whole body shook. Then there was a real warm feeling all through me to where my appendix was.

There were iron rails in front of this shadow of a person. I said I heard a deep small voice inside: "I want you to live." A shadow of a person with his arm straight up came closer and closer. Then there was a big flood of light coming in. I just cried like a baby. That warmth, beautiful warmth, inside of me. I can't really describe that beautiful warmth inside of me, just like a wave going through me.

Six months after the operation was done, because it was so dominate (sic) for me, I know there is something up there. I have that shadow of a person in my mind, and no one can take that away. It changed my life. I wanted to do good things. I didn't want to do bad things.

One could ask, did a guardian angel, an ancestor, or something else intervene to help this man? Whatever the case, this experience let him know that he was not alone.

In another case, a twenty-eight-year-old Caucasian mother of two reported sharing her personal space with another consciousness. The strange occurrence happened when she and her husband were relaxing together in a room in their home. Here's how she described it:

When I was wherever I was, I was very closely tangled up with someone else and communicating with them. Meanwhile, back on this plane, my husband and I were cuddled up very close and talking as well. So the best way I can describe it was that someone else was occupying his physical space in a spiritual sense. I also feel that somebody else was occupying my space... because somebody else was carrying on a conversation with my husband. So it was kind of like two separate sets of people kind of carrying on conversations but in the same space.

That was along the lines of the space-sharing thing, where I think it was two spirits were in my body and two spirits were in his body—not necessarily in the body but in the same space on different levels on different planes. Because when I came back and was talking to him later on about it, he was relaying a conversation he was having with me to which I was completely oblivious. So somebody or some entity was there, standing in for me and having a conversation with him. I don't know whether it was my subconscious or someone was kind of holding down the fort for me while I was off somewhere else.

History tells us that many famous people—including Charlemagne, Charles Dickens, Joan of Arc, John of the Cross, Mohandas Gandhi, René Descartes, Saint Francis of Assisi, Sigmund Freud, and William Blake—heard voices from invisible sources. Is it possible that people today may experience the same thing? The following account from an eight-year-old Caucasian female of Catholic faith raises that question. She reported that a foggy darkish blue shadow with droopy eyes had talked to her in her mind.

"If I told anyone she was in my mind, I had to be really bad and, like, be mean to my brother and sister," the girl said. "I had no clue why." Asked to clarify, she said, "If I don't be really bad, and if I tell everybody that she existed in my mind, she would harm my family or somebody I know or myself."

This girl was able to stop any further communications with the shadow by envisioning a protective bubble of white light around herself. Using white light for protection is both an ancient spiritual technique and similar to a modern psychology technique for creating a safe place. For this child and her family, there was no need to question whether the girl really had heard a shadow being speak to her. It was enough that the girl said the communication stopped after she used the bubble of white light.

People often describe changes in their consciousness and awareness as seeming to be the influence of an invisible being. These experiences can happen spontaneously, without any warning, and flow like a stream of consciousness that William James, the father of American psychology, spoke about. He warned that to take a segment of this flow out would not allow one to understand the wholeness of these phenomena. Do we really know all the origins of the thoughts that seem to enter our minds randomly?

To accurately perceive our universe is to recognize that there are influences in it other than ourselves. We must open up to the possibility that the universe holds more beings than just those we see, and we must protect ourselves from harmful invisible beings when necessary. We also must strive to understand and live with respect for other beings, including those we cannot see or interact with by ordinary means. All life must live in harmony, for if we damage the circle of life, we may very well threaten our own existence.

Reflections: Supernatural awareness allows you to connect to invisible beings that exist in our universe. When others validate your experiences, it becomes difficult to just write off the events as imagination or fantasy. To perceive and embrace unknown influences of your universe, you must open your mind and be willing to learn from others who can perceive more than you can.

Exercise: Have you had experiences where something outside of yourself has seemed to affect you? If so, make a list of the details of these experiences:

1. Did you experience physical sensations or bodily feelings?
2. Did you hear voices of something other than your own voice or thoughts in your mind?
3. Did you smell scents or odors not coming from a known source?
4. Anything else?

These questions may be difficult to answer, as our world is very thought and behaviorally focused, and what's affecting us can appear to come from other, more mundane areas of our experience. But it is worth carefully examining all the elements of the experience to discern which aspects of it may have come from a supernatural source.

Chapter 7

Perceiving Unexpected Beings and Objects

In this chapter, we will explore cases in which people perceived unexpected beings, objects, or phenomena. On the surface, their experiences may seem anomalous, deviating from the standard, normal, or expected ways of experiencing or perceiving something, and thus qualifying for the label "supernatural." The question is, did the people in these cases truly experience something *super*natural? Or did they, in fact, experience something that is completely natural, but not something we're used to experiencing because of our current ways of perceiving? In other words, what if our ways of perceiving are not, in fact, as limited as we, or our leaders and our science, currently believe? What new objects, entities, or phenomena could we encounter if our perception expanded even just a little bit—or even if we were open to the possibility of that expansion?

This first case comes from a forty-one-year-old, Italian engineer of Protestant faith. His experience happened around 1986 or 1987, in Milford, New Hampshire. He was about twenty years old at the time.

It was a Friday or Saturday night, sometime during the summer, and the weather was clear and warm. He, his girlfriend, and a friend were in his 1979 Camaro on their way back to his girlfriend's house at about midnight. He was driving, and his girlfriend was in the front passenger seat. Their friend was dozing in the back seat. They were driving down a very dark, two-way country road. There were no houses within a few miles. He was driving about thirty-five miles per hour up a slight hill that curved to the right.

What happened next didn't immediately register, and this total event was over in about ten seconds. He could see the roadway and trees ahead, illuminated as if there were an oncoming car. As they crested the hill, a glowing, bright white ball (about the size of a volleyball) headed towards them at very high speed. This white ball or orb followed the contour or path of the roadway, along the centerline and about four feet off the ground. He thought this white ball was, without a doubt, being intelligently controlled.

The orb was coming towards them, and as they were coming up over the hill, this orb and the car converged. The orb went over his car. It elevated itself over the car, following just above the car's profile. It was not like this ball just went up directly into space (or wherever). It was not like this orb went at a straight forty-five-degree angle. Instead, it followed the contours of his car's hood, windshield, and roof. The orb had been a few feet above the road, and it maintained that same few-feet distance above his car as it passed over.

This light from this ball quickly flooded the interior of his car. He glanced up at his rear-view mirror to catch it speeding in the opposite direction, continuing to follow the curves of the roadway. The road turned and went to the right as it crested the top of the hill. When he looked in his rear-view mirror, he observed that the ball turned, going to the left in his mirror, following the roadway. The orb quickly disappeared into the distance through the trees next to the roadway. It was gone in about two seconds. At this point, he was thinking to himself, "What the hell was that?" (In our interview, he said he probably did "that sideways head-tilt thing" and had an inquisitive look on his face when mentally asking himself that question.) He was like, "Wow, this was freaky."

If he had been alone, he probably would have completely disregarded this event and never committed it to memory. However, after a few seconds, as he was still trying to process what had just happened, he glanced over at his girlfriend. She was staring at him with an inquisitive, almost nervous look on her face. Before he could say anything, she said, "What was that?"

Their friend in the backseat hadn't even flinched but had slept through this whole event.

His girlfriend's house was only another few miles down the road. He dropped her and their friend off at their homes and went home to his parents' house, in Merrimack, for the night.

The next morning, he and his girlfriend spoke very briefly about this event but didn't really dwell on it. Though they had both acknowledged this event at the time it occurred, they never spoke of this orb again after that. He doesn't know if they both thought this orb was too bizarre to bring up in conversation, if they didn't want to let themselves believe what they had seen, or if they were satisfied that both of them had seen it. Perhaps the confirmation they had gotten from one another was sufficient enough for them to know in their own minds and hearts what had happened. Sometimes he still wonders if she ever thinks about that orb. If he ever sees her again, this orb will be the first thing he asks her about.

A side note about this case: There is such a thing as ball lightning, which appears as balls of light in various sizes, ranging from that of a ping-pong ball to that of a beach ball, and can be white, yellow, orange, red, or blue in color. This ball lightning is associated with thunderstorms and often moves erratically and disappears. However, the white ball of light this man saw did not move erratically or disappear. And he remembered no thunderstorm in the vicinity that day.

A ball of brilliant white light is central to a couple of interesting cases recorded by air-force pilot Martin Caidin in his book *Ghosts of the Air*.[7] On 7 September 1972, a pilot flying a passenger plane reported that a ball of white light with green and red flashes was following his aircraft. A radio operator also saw this light following the plane. Several years later, a student pilot in the same vicinity frantically reported to air traffic control that a white light was coming at his plane. The pilot and his plane then vanished and were never found.

This next experience with an unusual object was shared by a forty-eight-year-old Caucasian female with a high school diploma. She was also a military veteran.

This event happened on a warm summer night. She was probably eight or nine years old. Her mother had taken her grandmother home after the latter had had supper with them. Her father, a mechanic, was working in his garage. The girl decided to enjoy this summer night by lying out on a lawn chair and looking up at the stars. She closed her eyes for a few minutes until she noticed a faint humming sort of noise. It was very soft and steady. The noise was enough to make her open her eyes and say, "What is that?" The humming was faint, but just loud enough to prompt her to say, "Where is this coming from?"

It was quite a shock for this little girl to look up and see a huge, oval-kind-of-shaped silver object sitting or hovering just above the treetops. This object wasn't moving right, left, up, or down. It was just stopped in time, staying in one place above the tree level. She had seen things fly by and keep on going before, but she had never seen anything that would just sit there and just stay put in one spot.

This object didn't look round, but oval. (In our interview, she said she realized her description of "oval" and someone else's may be different.) To her, this object did have somewhat of an oval shape to it, but it was not elongated. Maybe it was more in between—not real round and not an elongated oval.

The object had red lights and some blue lights that went around it. It also had what looked like windows to her. These kind of square-type structures around the side of it appeared to have some sort of translucent (obviously not glass) something that went around this object. She could see these framed type of structures, but she could not see inside the object. The translucent structures weren't clear—not like a clear glass where you could look through and see anything. These structures just seemed to be there. What these structures were, she didn't know. They looked to her like they might have been a type of window. But who knows what those structures really were?

It took a few seconds for her to move; she stared at this object in disbelief for a few minutes. What is this thing? She didn't know what it was. She was in awe. She was like, "Oh my God, I couldn't imagine anything that big." This object's circumference was a large area. This object was probably a tractor-trailer length. She had never seen anything that big. Viewing this object shocked her because she knew it wasn't a plane. It didn't have any wings.

Being a small child, she felt scared at seeing something that big that didn't belong there. For her, "scared" was kind of like a shocked sort of feeling, kind of "freeze in one spot for a couple of seconds." Her heart was beating fast, and she felt adrenaline flowing through her. This fear came across, and her adrenaline started going, "Oh my God, what is this thing?"

Then she flew out of her lawn chair, took off, and headed into her dad's garage, which was very close by, to try to get him to come see this object. She was dancing, jumping up and down, yelling, "Daddy, there's something in the sky! You have to see it. There's this big silver thing in the sky. Hurry up! Come on!"

Her father responded, "What? I'm underneath the car. What are you talking about?"

She said, "Dad, you have to come see it."

She didn't know how to describe this object to her father. She thought if she could have gotten him out of there, then he would have seen it for himself. She didn't give him much of a description other than it was silver and in the sky.

But the object was gone when her father got out there. By the time she dragged him out of that garage, there was nothing there, which made her look foolish. Because she was a little girl, her father just saw her actions as ridiculous and just went back to his business.

He said, "I don't see anything." He looked up at the sky where she was pointing and looked back at her. "There's nothing there. What are you talking about?" She tried to explain to him what she had seen. She was all excited and talking fast. He kind of laughed or chuckled at her. "Oh, okay, yeah," he said. He looked at her and then just kind of shook his head. Then he went back into his garage.

Her dad just didn't ask for any more detail. He did not ask, "What did you think you saw?" He didn't ask her anything. She thought he believed she must have imagined the whole thing. She took his time, and then he went back under his car.

She just stood there. She looked at where the object had been, and she looked around her. There was nothing there. She didn't remember where she went at that point or what she did after that.

She had seen this object in her mind for the past forty years of her life. In her mind, it was still there. This experience was something she had kept inside of her. She didn't know if she had told her husband, whom she had been with for years, about it. Even as a teenager, she had kept this experience to herself. This event was something she could still see today (in her mind). This occurrence was still so clear. She used to wonder, "Was this event real? Or was something wrong with me?" For her, (the memory of) this experience has never changed.

In some cases, the unusual thing someone saw was less like an inanimate object and more like an animated being, albeit one that can't be categorized as an angel, demon, or other recognizable supernatural being. This next example is from a twenty-eight-year-old, French-Canadian, single female artist. She had a bachelor's degree in fine art and was of the pagan faith.

She had just graduated from her senior year of college and had a night job cleaning offices at a healthcare center. One night she cleaned the neurology center and then went to the cardiac center. In the latter, she said, there was one weird thing that would happen: the lights were automatic and usually turned on when someone walked under them. That night, some of these lights were turning off instead of on when she walked under them, but she sort of dismissed this anomaly.

She went about cleaning and mopping a bathroom. When she came out of this bathroom, she felt a weird buzz around her head. It was like she had a TV on her head. There was a weird white-noise buzzing all around her face and her neck, and it felt sort of prickly on her skin.

She also felt like something was watching her. So she looked up, and there was this weird creature on the ceiling. She averted her eyes quickly. It was hard to describe, but this being looked like a mass of black, without a comprehensible shape or form, and was almost crouching on the ceiling, defying gravity. She didn't get a great look at it because this creature freaked her out.

She was just like, "Okay, I am going to quickly finish this job." So she skipped the vacuuming and went and sat in the cafeteria. She didn't think there was anyone else in the building. She was not ready to clock out quite yet. She was just waiting around.

She was feeling freaked out and frightened. Then she felt that high-frequency buzzing feeling again around her head, neck, shoulders, and back.

Feeling really nervous and weird, she called her friend Amos. As they were talking, she told him that she had seen the creature. Suddenly, there was very real static interference over the phone. It sounded like when a radio gets static interference. It was loud enough that she couldn't hear Amos talk for a few moments.

Then she saw the same creature scuttle quickly down the hall in a weird, lopsided shuffle movement. It looked like sort of a 3D silhouette—all this compressed black smoke in one area or a lack of light hiding this area. It was just really a dark shadow that almost had a mass to it, like its form was made out of a black shadowy or smoky sort of thing. This being had the torso of a human, and the back legs looked like those of a scrawny, emaciated dog. This creature had no head. Its front legs were really tiny and skinny and almost more attached to the chest than to where the shoulders would be. And because the back legs were bigger than the front ones, it sort of moved like a dog, but really awkwardly, in a quick, chopped up shuffle.

Seeing it again, she kind of freaked out. The static on her phone stopped.

"Are you okay? That was really static interference," Amos said. He started laughing at that situation.

"Yeah, I'm leaving," she decided. She clocked out and left. She went home, and that was the end of that for the night.

The next day she came into work. She was in the kitchen during her little self-appointed break, eating a little bit of dinner, when all of a sudden, there was all this banging on the cabinets and the walls, and the TV turned on. Thinking the creature had returned, she started yelling at it. She wanted to make this thing stop. She thought she probably looked really silly, but she said, "Leave me alone! You're not allowed to do this. You can only talk to me on my time, when I say it is okay. You have to stop doing this because I don't like it. I am going to ignore you if you keep doing this. I am not going to give you any attention. Just go away."

Then this creature stopped, for the most part. Or it stopped bothering her at work, anyway. Weeks later, she saw this creature again, this time at her boyfriend's house while they were eating dinner. She just saw it really quickly in another room.

The third and last time she saw it, she was with her boyfriend (whom she wasn't dating at the time) and her friend Amos (whom she had called on the phone the first time she had seen the creature). One night, the three of them were doing some urban exploration, which is when you go into abandoned houses or weird construction sites and just explore them. They were going to explore some little pipeline that was being made near a large store. She wasn't really dressed for the occasion, so she said, "I'll just sit out here and make sure nobody comes around and gets us in trouble or whatever."

The whole location looked like a construction site. Both the large store and the pipeline, or whatever they were building, were up on a hill. And the pipeline was sort of underground. To get to it, you had to go down a ladder. Her boyfriend and Amos went down into the pipeline to check it out. This area around this location had piles and piles of dirt, and the places in between were flat. There were construction vehicles hanging around.

She saw the creature again—just kind of like there, not very close to her, not as close as it had been previously. She had that weird fuzzy feeling again too. And that was all. She hadn't seen the creature again since then.

The creature this woman described resembles one another person told me about anecdotally. This man's unusual encounter began with him hearing the sound of clothes snapping—like the sound laundry makes when it is shaken out. He heard the clothes-snap sound, and then he saw a black thing. It looked like it had been curled up and dropped, he said. This black thing was a foot away from his bed and four feet off the ground. That was the first time he saw the black thing. The second time he saw it, he decided to develop an understanding with it. "I don't bother you, and you don't bother me," he told it. "If it happens again, I'm going to have to ask you to leave." He never saw that black thing again.

Here's a third example of an encounter with an unusual, unrecognizable being. When a twenty-five-year-old woman was having sex with her boyfriend, she would avoid completing the sex act because, she said, she would see this horrific creature as she came close. Her boyfriend decided to fix this situation. The next time they had sex, he pushed her through to completion, only to see the same horrific creature she had described. Several times after that event, he heard the creature breathing by the side of her bed. He began to utilize a white-light protection technique described in my book *Perceptual Hypnosis*, and these supernatural manifestations subsided and did not reoccur.[8]

Hopefully, these examples make you consider what else might exist in our world beyond our usual ways of perceiving. These cases also raise some interesting questions: When people see unusual balls of light, inexplicable objects in the air, or strange, unidentifiable beings, are they creating these things themselves? Are these phenomena created by the thoughts of others? Or are they independent entities existing in their own right? If they are independent entities, could such creatures come from other planets, other universes, or other times or dimensions? How can earthly beings be the only beings that exist in an infinite universe?

We humans certainly have imaginations that create projections. Psychotic perceptions are based in fantasy and illusion. Yet not all unusual perceptions are psychotic. We still have not learned to completely distinguish real from unreal in the universe. With all our scientific advances, the greatest tool of supernatural awareness we have is our own being, which most of us are still learning to fully utilize.

Reflections: There are many unexplained objects and beings in the world. If these things exist, we cannot dismiss them simply by believing they don't exist.

In addition to appearing to us in real life, as illustrated in this chapter's cases, unusual objects and beings may appear in your dreams and imaginations. When these things are healthy and helpful, they will bring positive experiences and connections to your life. They may also warn you and protect you from negative experiences. During transitions, unusual creatures may appear to herald in a change or, conversely, attempt to scare you back into complacency and your safety zone. If these objects or entities appear to be harmful or destructive, then you need to protect yourself or seek help from spiritually gifted healers, medical professionals, and mental health professionals, depending on your individual case.

Unusual supernatural creatures are often only glimpsed briefly. If these creatures or entities are bothersome, talking to them often seems to stop further incidents. Often the results of the interaction are undeniable and hard to dismiss.

Exercise: How can you distinguish what is a true and real experience with a supernatural object or entity from one that is not? Here are a few questions that can help:

1. How would you describe the unusual object, being, or creature? Describe it in detail.
2. Is it or your experience with it burned in your memory in a way that makes it more prominent than most memories?
3. What did that experience mean or do for you in your life? What was the outcome?

Chapter 8

Communicating after Death

Throughout history there have been stories proving to individuals that communication between people can continue after one of them has died and that death is not an ending but a new beginning. In a number of my cases, individuals reported being in a shared space while communicating with someone who had died. In this chapter I share a few of these experiences in great detail. A prevalent characteristic in these stories seems to be a unity between us and the universe: cases in which someone is able to communicate with loved ones who have recently died suggests that some connection continues to exist between us and our loved ones even after death. Apparently, something more is going on beyond our physical measurable existence. Each case in this chapter also includes elements of other types of supernatural experiences pointed out in earlier chapters.

The first case is from a forty-two-year-old, divorced Jewish female. She had a bachelor of science in the arts and was a musician and educator. She described having a spiritual, energetic relationship with her unborn child; that relationship continued even after the child died four days after birth.

During her first pregnancy, this woman was living in Israel. Occasionally, she said, you would find cats and kittens wandering around the area where she lived. One day early in her pregnancy (two or three months), she looked outside through her porch window and saw a dead little black kitten there. She felt this kitten was some kind of sign, and she knew that her baby was not going to survive. Just seeing a little baby kitten dead at her doorstep was sort of a premonition telling her that this baby was not going to survive in the physical world. However, she never voiced her observation to anyone.

(She never had a kitten die on her doorstep before or after this experience.)

During her pregnancy, she felt an energetic connection with her baby as the child grew inside of her. She felt a relationship with her baby. She didn't know if that relationship was the same thing other mothers feel. To her, this relationship wasn't just as if there were a body inside of her. It was an energetic experience—an energetic relationship with this fetus that was growing inside of her. She didn't ask to know the baby's gender prior to birth, but she always knew her baby was a girl.

This pregnancy was fine until her fifth month, when things began going wrong. Her medical professionals said her baby and placenta weren't growing as they should be.

In the sixth month she was admitted to a hospital for a month of bed rest and to be monitored. She experienced this hospital as anything but a restful place. It was a horrible, stressful experience. After a month there, she was sent home.

In her seventh month, she went to the doctor for a regular checkup. Her baby was in distress, and she was taken to the hospital. There was a lot of scurrying going on around her, and then she was taken in for an emergency cesarean section (C-section) because the medical professionals thought her baby was in danger. She was not awake for her baby's birth because she was under anesthesia. Later, she opened her eyes and saw a group of family members all standing around her bed, looking at her. She was groggy. These family members told her that she had had a baby girl. Her premature baby was not with her in her hospital room, but was in an incubator, hooked up to monitors, in the neonatal section of the intensive care unit (ICU).

Her baby was very tiny and lived in this world for four days. The woman was brought into the ICU in a wheelchair to visit her baby a few times. She couldn't remember if she held her baby on these visits, but she saw her baby in the incubator. The baby looked stressed, as "all these medical things" were attached to her, and was breathing quickly. She was probably the size of the woman's hand, not much bigger. And her baby was struggling. It was nice to see her baby's physical presence, to see her baby physically, to get to know her and know this was a real thing that had happened. But seeing her baby struggle was difficult. Not being able to touch her baby and be with her physically was also difficult, although she didn't think about this difficulty at the time.

On the fourth day, she was in her room, lying in her bed, when she felt a presence. She felt that there was something swirling up above her, diagonally to her left. This presence was between her bed and the door, up in the left corner of the room. She looked up and saw an energy swirling overhead, at the end of her bed, near the doorway and slightly above her. She sensed and saw this energy. In our interview, she said she could still see the energy in her mind's eye. If she had to draw it, this energy would look like a spirally thing, like how a storm with an eye might be depicted in a weather report. This energy was spinning, but not as dramatically as a spiraling storm front. It was just a swirling energy, going round and round, clockwise, toward the right. Its quickly spinning gave it a cloudy white appearance.

She watched this energy and *knew* it was her baby's spirit.

She thought that her baby had died or was dying, one or the other, and had come to say goodbye, had come to be with her. She was actually happy and enjoyed this swirling energy because she felt that her baby was close. At the same time, she was upset because she wanted to be with her baby. So she was kind of confused and didn't really know what was happening. Everything happened so fast; she doesn't know how long that presence remained because she lost awareness of linear clock time. But she remembered that it was a happy moment. The swirling energy made her feel good.

She didn't know exactly what her baby was telling her, but she felt that her baby was happy. And she was happy that her baby was happy. She felt good, and she wanted to be in that happiness. It seemed like her baby wanted her mother and herself to be happy and not struggling, because the pregnancy had been a struggle, her birth had been a struggle, her physical existence was a struggle. But with her energy, on the energy plane, all was good.

At some point, the woman's mother-in-law walked in the door, and the woman noticed her in a second. She also noticed her mother-in-law's face; she didn't look happy. The swirling thing vanished in a flash—just went away. The way the energy vanished could be compared to a cartoon, like how a cartoon character quickly runs away or flies off, and you sort of see this dust or something like that. It was as if this swirling energy was interrupted by her mother-in-law's appearance, and just "fsssh," it went away in a flash. The woman was taken aback because she wanted to continue being with that spirit. She had been enjoying that swirling presence. She wanted to be there longer and was upset that her mother-in-law had walked in at that moment and interrupted her time together with her baby.

Her mother-in-law started talking, and the woman knew what she was going to tell her: her daughter had already passed. She didn't really want her mother-in-law to tell her that because she already knew her daughter died. And she could see on her mother-in-law's face that she was clearly struggling with how to tell her. Her mother-in-law just sort of said, "Well, she died." Then the woman just sat there silently, because she was still in that place with her baby's spirit.

She doesn't remember how long her mother-in-law stayed in her room or what occurred after that. She just remembered being brought to the ICU to see her baby's little body all wrapped up in a blanket. They brought her in to see her baby one more time and to say goodbye. She remembered looking at this nurse holding her little tiny baby. This nurse was holding her baby in a loving embrace, and her baby looked happy, peaceful, and content. She thinks the nurse asked her if she wanted to hold her baby. She did not. She was content just to look at her baby. She remembered feeling happy that her baby looked so peaceful and content.

At that time, she didn't know much about having a baby or being a mother or about death, burial, and mourning. She was told that her baby would be buried in a grave with another who would protect her soul. She didn't remember very clearly, but she was told that a traditional burial would not take place because her baby was still considered a fetus. She trusted her baby was being taken care of properly and according to her religious tradition and didn't feel any need to ask any questions. She did not know where her baby was buried and never felt a need to know. Her baby had always been an energy to her, and she knew her baby would always be with her.

She had to stay in that hospital for a week or so, which was a terrible time for her. She was moved to a section where there were other women who had given birth and were with their babies. She was later moved to a room with other women who, like her, had suffered a loss. She remembered crying all the time because she was empty-handed. She had no baby to hold. She just felt physical and emotional pain and emptiness—lots of emptiness. She cried uncontrollably—so much.

What can she say about that, as a woman? She was pregnant, and she was carrying this fetus. She was supposed to come out of this experience with a physical thing, a baby, and she didn't have her baby. So she couldn't hold her daughter in her arms. She couldn't feel her there. Her baby was no longer in her womb, but her baby wasn't in her arms. So her arms felt empty, and she felt empty because she had lost her baby. She had spent seven months with her baby inside her. She had experienced this supernatural experience, or whatever you wanted to call this energy exchange. It had been her expectation that she was going to have something physical to come home with, and she didn't, so she was empty all around. Both her baby and her baby's energy had vanished. She was empty completely.

She was finally released from the hospital and returned home. She remembered her arms feeling empty and useless. She was home and alone. Even her baby's little spirit had gone. She could not feel her baby's spirit there anymore. She knew only one thing for sure: that she was going to allow herself whatever time she needed to mourn and to heal. It took her a year.

In the next case, a woman perceived a change in her space as she interacted, on two different occasions, with deceased relatives. This forty-three-year-old divorced woman was of English and Danish descent. She had a doctorate degree in medicine and was functioning as a clinical director at a medical center in New England.

The first occurrence happened when she was eight years old. Stephen, her older cousin, had just died in a motorcycle accident. She was by herself in the bedroom she shared with her sister, lying in bed but not sleeping. All of a sudden, her dead cousin was just there in her room. He was standing by her sister's vanity, which had a tri-mirror on it. She could not only see him standing there but also see him reflected in those mirrors. She remembered accepting that he was there, but she also wondered how he could be there. She was sure her cousin was in her room, yet contradictorily, she also wasn't really sure he was. It was seeing his reflection in her sister's mirrors that made her believe he really was present.

He was also touching things. She could hear him picking up her sister's hairbrushes and things; that sound drew her attention to him. It was not like she could hear the sounds with her ears. It was more like almost hearing them in her head. Those sounds let her know he was there or that his presence was real, giving her a sense like she was with him in her room and that they were together there in that space.

Her cousin said something, and then he walked over to the other side of her room, near her bed, where she was. She remembered he had on a red shirt. To her, that was one of the most striking things about the experience. Red was Stephen's favorite color. And because red was his favorite color, red was her favorite color as well.

Her cousin stood there and looked at her. He said, "It's all okay. It's going to be okay."

She had always been able to remember this occurrence so clearly. It was like she and Stephen were not really in her room but in a separate, shared space. She remembered thinking the whole time, "Why is he, like, talking to me?" But it was him. There was nothing about this image or this person that was not him. She accepted that it was Stephen. It was Stephen standing there and Stephen talking to her and Stephen moving from the vanity to the side of her bed. She never felt afraid. She never felt like this wasn't happening. She never questioned his presence.

There was never any point that she had been asleep and then woke up and said, "Oh, my God." He was there, he said what he said, and then he just walked back and wasn't there anymore. His presence was something she could still see. She had never really talked about this occurrence to a lot of people, so conveying this feeling was a hard thing to do without sounding like she was all over the place. She didn't know how to explain it. It was like they were in her room because everything was there that was her room. Yet it was also like she and her cousin were talking in a different way, on a different level, than just in her room. Her cousin had actually died in an accident that same day she saw him, so there was no way he could have gotten up in her room.

She didn't remember anything else, like her cousin coming to give her a message. She hadn't told anybody about the experience for years, because, first, her cousin's mother had lost her mind and was really not nice to all of her family afterwards. Her aunt had told them that they should be lucky they are alive because Stephen was dead, and he was the best of them. She knew that she couldn't say anything to her aunt because this aunt would probably slap her or make her sit over in a corner and recite one hundred "Hail Marys." Second, she had grown up with an alcoholic father and an enabler mother, and they didn't really teach or encourage her and her cousin to be close to each other. She knew if she said anything about her dead cousin's presence, she would probably get ridiculed and teased about it. There was a four-year gap between her three older siblings and her brother and herself. No matter what she would say to her siblings, they would treat her like she was a dumb child who didn't know anything. She felt that if she said anything, it was going to bring ridicule or shame, or she would be told, "Don't talk about that because Stephen is dead. There is no way that happened to you. You were just dreaming. That could not have happened."

There wasn't anybody she felt like she could talk to about this experience with her cousin. Plus, it also felt like the experience was personal to her—like her cousin had come to her for a specific reason, whatever that was. Even though she never told anyone about it, and to this day she really didn't know why he did, her cousin *did* communicate with her, and she had thought about that communication over the years.

On the second occasion she communicated with a deceased relative, this woman was twenty-three or twenty-four. Her dad was sick with cancer. She was at the house she was renting with her brother. During her experience with Stephen, she had not been asleep, but just lying in her bed. This time, she was alone in her house and sleeping. She felt somebody there in her room with her. She could always kind of tell when someone was around her and was hyperaware of noises or movements. She said her feeling at the time seemed very similar to what you typically feel when you feel somebody in the room with you.

All of a sudden, she just knew her father was there, without any question. She described it as "almost the same kind of feeling when you are somewhere and you know someone is watching you or looking at you." She sensed a presence and didn't feel afraid. To her, his presence was "like a person was standing in your room, and you would look up at them and go, 'What are you doing in my room?'" His presence gave her that strong of a feeling. The feeling wasn't like, "Oh god, I'm dreaming." She had felt someone in her room and woken up.

She didn't question, "Why is he in my room?" even though she knew he was in the hospital. Her father was just standing there, and she knew he was there to see her. It was not like he brought her to some other place; he was there, and she could sense him. (She noted that it was a tough feeling to describe.)

Her father was standing in her really small room. It had once been a sun porch, and it was just big enough for her bed and bureau. She and her father were speaking but not with words. It was like they could talk, but she wasn't actually talking to him. Like Stephen, her father also said that "it was going to be okay," he was alright now, and she shouldn't worry about him.

She thought, "Oh, my father is dead. He must have died." Then she fell back to sleep. Later that morning, her oldest brother called and told her that their father had died. She knew that she had seen Stephen after he had died. But she didn't know if she perceived her father before or around the time that he had died. She never thought to ask that question at that moment either. She didn't tell anybody about that event right away, either, because this occurrence felt like a personal experience with him.

Her father had come to her—"for whatever reason he had to do that"—but why she didn't really know. At first he was just talking to her, and then it was like he was watching her and there was no fanfare about it. Her experience of her father's presence wasn't a dream; it was like he was really there. The presence was him. She felt that if she had reached out, she probably could have touched him. "You know how when you are with someone," she said. "You know their essence. You know their smell or the way they make you feel." His presence was just that kind of a thing.

She didn't remember any other real details other than when she woke up later, she knew he died and then learned that he had, in fact, died.

She remembered thinking of this second encounter, "Oh my gosh! That was like what happened with Stephen." It was the same feeling, she said: "Like you are there together. You are in that room. You are not in a bubble, and you are in a different space in time inside that room." That was what she meant about both occurrences being similar.

When Stephen had appeared to her, it was like he was there with her—not that he had a message, but he had come to her. Even at the time, as a child, she felt like he had come to her for a reason. She just immediately accepted his presence; it didn't scare her. It was like she and Stephen were "inside space and time," which, she noted, sounded like a strange phrasing. But it was like they were there together, doing this transaction engagement, yet they weren't part of everything else that was going on around them. It was just them and their communication and that was it. She and her cousin were there together for a reason, though whatever the reason was she didn't know. This togetherness was a hard thing to describe, because it was nothing that they touched. She could only explain how that togetherness felt: it felt like him and her and nothing else, although she knew she was in her room. Her focus was just the energy or the thing they were having together.

In the second experience, with her father, she felt a presence, like when somebody comes up behind you slowly, and you go, "Woo, I didn't know you were there!" It was almost like she and her father weren't there, and then all of a sudden her father was there and saying something to her. She had to listen. She could feel him in her and around her, yet she could see his presence too. It was the same way with Stephen. She thinks the biggest connection with a presence was that feeling of, "Oh, Stephen's here. Or Father's here to tell me something. He wants me to know something or he came to me."

It was like they almost had no place else to go. Years after the visits, she thought, "Why would both of them come to me and be so similar in feeling and the way we interacted and the whole thing?" Perhaps her cousin and her father had felt there was no place else to go. Or perhaps they knew she would be there, ready or open.

She didn't know what the right word would be to describe these experiences with her cousin and her father. The visits definitely were real; they weren't dreams or hallucinations. The togetherness she had felt with them was actually more tangible than what she felt sitting there with me (in our interview). She couldn't feel my presence within her, yet when her cousin and father appeared, she could feel their presences within her. I, her interviewer, was separate from her, even though we were in the same space. But her cousin and father were almost part of her.

She used to keep journals and diaries, especially when she was a child. She threw them away at one point, and she wished now that she had kept them because she was sure she had written a lot of this stuff down. Her family was very dysfunctional, and she never felt that she could tell anybody anything about her feelings or the things that happened to her. "That is part of that ridicule thing," she said. Even as a child, she knew "you don't go off on different topics; you just don't talk about certain things." If she described these presences to her family, they definitely would have been, "You are a crazy child. Get out of here." So she wished she still had those books and could see what she wrote about her experiences with her cousin and her father at the time, as her outlet for everything was writing.

A different example of material evidence validating a supernatural experience came from a fifty-two-year-old married woman with a bachelor's of arts degree and no religious affiliation. She and her family had been searching for months for an important insurance document and finally gave it up for lost. Weeks afterwards, after this woman had forgotten about the search, she went to bed at her usual time, without any changes in routine. At some point in the night, she awakened, but did not open her eyes right away. She felt as though someone was in the room with her, and she wasn't sure whom it could be. She lived with two grown sons, and her first thought was that one of them had come in to get a book and didn't want to wake her. As the minutes passed, she knew it was not one of her sons. There was just a sense that "someone" was in the room—a presence. Sensing a presence is hard to describe if you've never had this kind of experience. To her, sensing a presence was like a sense that blind people develop—a kind of prickling of the senses, a vague feeling of danger, though you can't see anything. She also compared it to the sensation one might feel when someone is looking at you. Say you're staring at the back of someone's head, in church or a similar setting; in a short time, they will often sense that you are looking at them and will look back to see who is behind them.

She began to get really nervous and wondered what to do. If it wasn't one of her sons, was it a burglar or other intruder? She then asked herself, *Should I scream, hoping to scare this intruder, or fake sleep and hope that they will just go away?*

As quickly as this fear came it disappeared, and she was just puzzled. One minute she was fearful, the next minute she wasn't—much the same way someone might feel when they've seen a person take off a horror mask. Once the fear passed, for some reason it did not seem unusual to see her father there. She couldn't explain why, but her father put her at ease. Then she smelled his pipe tobacco as if he were in her room, smoking. There was no doubt about that; the smell was her father's favorite tobacco flavor, "rum." That particular brand and flavor had not been sold for years.

This woman turned towards the wall at the opposite end of her room, where her closet was, and once she opened her eyes, it was obvious that no one was standing at that wall. Yet she still had this feeling that someone was in her room. The only other place they would have been was by the wall behind her. When she turned toward it, "My dad was standing near the door, just as though he had dropped in for a visit, smoking his Kaywoodie pipe."

She asked him, "How have you been?" and sat up at the edge of her bed. Her father was about six feet tall and very distinguished looking. He said, "You chaps are all looking in the wrong places for that bloody paper, you know." By now her initial fear had passed, the experience seemed normal, and she felt very relaxed. She said to him, "Naturally, only you would know where to look." He told her to go to the desk upstairs and find a particular coin saver of his. The missing insurance paper was in that coin saver.

She then asked him if her deceased mother was around. Her father said he didn't know her mother's whereabouts just then. Regarding coming back, he said he was allowed this trip, but didn't know how "they" worked things yet. He said that he had to leave, repeated his description of the coin saver, and then said, "Remember, thoughts are things." The woman turned away for a split second to lean on her pillow, and when she turned back, her father was gone.

This event had happened so quickly that she doubted her experience was real. Then she got scared. The impact of what had happened hit her, and trying to rationalize it was impossible.

She began wondering about the experience's greater implications. For instance, if her father could drift in and out of this dimension, could others, who were not so good, do the same? In other words, might she expect a visit from an evil person? What could she or anyone do if an evil person, rather than a friendly relative, "came through" to visit? Could they physically hurt us? Could they influence us? Is "possession" real? She had lots to think about.

She also wondered whether she had been asleep or dreaming. Sometimes, she said, when awaking from a deep sleep, don't you wonder whether you had been dreaming or having a real experience, such as, "Did I really hear the phone?"

In any case, several days later, she went to her father's house and looked for the coin saver. There was the insurance document! Then she believed that her experience, though mysterious, was real. She didn't fully understand how such things happen, but some communication really took place, as was evidenced by the recovered papers.

She said she thought that we operate on AM frequency. When we pass over, we go to FM, if that explains what she thinks happens when we die. Actually, she thinks that our energy or life force or soul goes into another plane right beside this level of existence. She thought some can pass back and forth, others cannot. But then she would have to say that she was on AM and her father left FM to visit AM. Her father was just there, slightly wavy, but there, and then her father wasn't there. The weird thing is that the waviness did not seem unusual to her. She explained wavy as the way one sees heat rise from the street. She described it just after her father had gone, experiencing a kind of amazement, wondering whether or not to tell anyone, "lest they think I had been drinking!" She did tell her sons the next day, and her sons were not as skeptical as she thought they would be. She expected them to say, "Yeah right, Mom!" But no, in fact, her sons had also felt their grandpa's presence from time to time, and still do. They are engineers and usually need positives or experimental results to prove the presence of something. In real time, this experience of her father may have been seven or ten seconds. This event took much longer to describe for something that was over so quickly.

This next case comes from a sixty-one-year-old Protestant mother with a master's degree in accounting. Her grandmother, who had been more like a mother to her than her own mother, had died around 1985. It was not that her own mother was neglectful, the woman said, but her grandmother was very forceful and kind of pushed her mother out of the way. Before her grandmother died, she'd had congenital heart failure and was sick for quite some time.

"I want you to know that if you don't see me after I die, there's no life after death whatsoever," her grandmother told her, "because I'm coming back."

The woman said she kind of blew off that statement because her grandmother was a very determined woman, and most of what she told her granddaughter either came from her determination or was a tall tale instead of the truth. For example, her grandmother told her ex-husband, who was really superstitious and believed in ghosts, that when she died she was coming back to haunt him. He hadn't seen her grandmother, so the woman had just taken her grandmother's promise to visit after death in the same light as all the other things her grandmother said.

She was very emotional when her grandmother died. Her grandmother had been like an appendage in her life. It was very difficult even for her to explain their relationship. Sometimes her grandmother was very controlling. She always wanted to tell her granddaughter what she should be doing, and she, the granddaughter, kind of rebelled.

Her doctors had told her grandmother, who was eighty-eight, that she wasn't in the position to receive a replacement heart or have anything else done for her. The woman had been very upset when her grandmother told her that, because she interpreted it as her grandmother saying, "If I could just lay down here on the couch and close my eyes and never wake up, I would be very happy." When she called her grandmother on her poor attitude toward her health and told her how unfair that was, her grandmother propped herself up by the elbow and said, "Look, I'm eighty-eight years old. I have had two husbands, six children, fifteen grandchildren, thirty great-grandchildren, and been through two wars, a world conflict, and every invention known in your lifetime. I am tired. I have had enough."

On the day her grandmother died, there were family members in the house taking care of her. As they went out to work, they said goodbye, but her grandmother didn't wake up. They just thought she didn't respond because she was asleep on the couch. But when her aunt went down to make her breakfast, her grandmother was dead.

Her grandmother's death altered their family stability. It was kind of like a rug was pulled out from underneath them. Her mom even said to her, "She was a really effective mother." Her grandmother had raised her when she was little. Her mother had been divorced, and they had moved in with her grandmother. Then, when her mother had remarried, they moved two houses down the street. She was always at her grandmother's house. It really was kind of a surprise when her grandmother died. She would think, "Well, maybe she is coming back." She had some anger issues to discuss with her grandmother. She also felt that her grandmother had just given up instead of sticking it out and trying to live longer.

This woman had a friend, a young woman about her age, who was the minister of their church. After her grandmother died, the two of them went out to dinner. This minister friend wanted to see how she was doing. When she explained what her grandmother had said before she died, her minister got very defensive and very upset. The minister told her that her grandmother had no business telling her that she would come back. No one has come back from the dead to say what's happened, this minister said. So we don't know what happens when we die. It was not really fair for her grandmother to have put that false hope in her head.

A couple of months went by, and the woman was still very mournful about losing her grandmother. She was living in her own apartment, and she usually slept with her bedroom door open. One night, out of the clear blue, she just woke up—just completely woke up. It wasn't that she'd had a bad dream; it wasn't that she'd heard a noise. She was just wide awake.

She glanced out into her living room, where there was a lamp and an end table. Standing there was a silhouette of a man—a big, heavyset man with a big broad-rim farmer's hat, suspenders, and overalls. She could see the outline of boots on his feet. He was just a silhouette—just the side of him—and he was just standing there. She kept blinking her eyes, thinking she was half asleep and what she saw wasn't really there. Then he turned his head towards her. She looked right at him, and he completely vanished, like smoke. It was as if she were half asleep and what she'd seen was just maybe the streetlight and other lights from outside playing a game on her.

About two nights later, she woke up exactly the same way. There was no dream, no noise, nothing. She was just suddenly awake. This time, there was an older lady standing over her bed. ("Older" meaning "grandmother style.") This older lady had on a high-waist skirt, and a long-sleeved shirt with puffy arms and a waistline that came up under her breasts. She could tell this old lady was overweight because her bosom was very full. Her hair was in a bun pulled back on her head. She was standing there with her arms crossed, just looking at her.

The woman sat up in bed and thought, "Okay, I have to make sure I'm awake, and I'll stand up." As she stood up, this older lady stayed there. She started to get a little nervous. She didn't know what to expect. But then she asked herself, "Do I feel fear here?" At first, she was a little scared of the unknown, but then she thought it was not making her feel afraid. This older woman did the same thing the man she'd seen in her living room had done: she just vanished.

At this point, the woman was dating her soon-to-be husband, and she explained these presences to him. Her fiancé didn't think she was crazy, but he hadn't seen anything. Everyone kept saying to her these encounters were the result of "an emotional occurrence," meaning, they happened because she had recently lost the grandmother she had been so attached to. They had been so close; no one really could understand the relationship that she and her grandmother had had. Her grandmother had been obsessed with running her life. And she and her grandmother were involved with each other "all the way." She thought what her friends said about her experiences of the ghosts made sense. But her fiancé said to her, "I really believe you. I believe what you're saying to me," and she was thankful someone believed her.

She kept thinking she must be losing her mind. Her family was telling her, "Oh, it's just your mind playing tricks on you because you really miss Grandma. You know what Grandma said to you. So intelligently, your mind is making this up so whatever she told you would be right." But she didn't know those people who appeared in her living room. She had never seen those people in her life.

She and her fiancé had made plans to go to Walt Disney World in Florida. One night when they were there, her fiancé got up to go to the bathroom. All of the lights were out in the room. He went to the bathroom, did his thing, and came back out. He turned around to turn off the bathroom light, and he saw someone standing there. It was a man, not heavyset, but with big, baggy jeans or pants on, and a heavy coat. This man was just standing there over the bed, looking at her. Her fiancé told her, "I kind of squinted my eyes again, and that man was still there. I went to turn out the light, and again I looked and just like you said, that man turned to look at me. And he evaporated just like smoke—gone."

The next morning her fiancé said again, "I saw exactly what you were talking about when I came out of the bathroom. I went to turn around to shut the light off in the bathroom. I looked into the other room, and sure enough, there was someone standing over the bed looking at you. And he just turned and looked at me and disappeared." So she thought, "Well, maybe it is not me imagining things. Maybe those apparitions are really true." She must have asked him twelve times during the day, "Are you just saying this to make me feel better, really?" He responded, "No, I'm telling you, Molly. I saw what you saw, I'm telling you what you described I've seen."

After their trip to Walt Disney World was over, they went down to Fort Myers to see her older cousin, who had a home there. She explained her situation to her cousin.

This cousin had lost a son from a medical problem and kept saying to her, "You know, I was a nurse, and the mind can really play big tricks on you. If you're seeing these people, why haven't I seen my son who died? He's never come back to talk to me. I've never seen him."

"I don't know," the woman replied. "Maybe you just don't believe that it's possible, and that's kind of a barrier."

"Oh no, this is foolishness," her cousin said.

When the woman and her fiancé had arrived at her cousin's house, there were a couple of other cousins there too. One of them was her cousin's younger sister, who was very spiritual. When they were growing up, this sister had done a lot of astrology chart readings and "all this other stuff." She would read people's charts and talk about things that would happen and things that had happened, and a lot of those things came true, the woman said. Her younger cousin was one of the few people in her family who believed what she was telling her about her supernatural experiences. This cousin believed some sort of force was trying to communicate with her.

That night, they were all going to bed, and her younger cousin and she were sharing a room with twin beds. Her younger cousin said to her, "Look, if you see something, wake me up, will you?" She said, "Okay," and went to bed.

Again, out of the clear blue, she woke up during the night. She looked over, and there was a young woman, maybe in her twenties, with long hair, sitting at the edge of her cousin's bed. This young woman was leaning over with her elbow on her knee and her hand on her chin. She was just sitting there, looking at her. She knew this young woman had long hair because she could see it all falling forward.

She sat up and said to her cousin, "Kimmy, hurry up! Kimmy, there is one there." She could only hear her cousin snoring. She kept saying, "Kimmy, wake up! She's there." Then the young woman lifted her head off her palm, turned and looked at her, looked at her cousin, and vanished, just like the other ones—just smoke, just gone.

The next morning, she told her younger cousin about seeing this young woman. Her cousin was disappointed she had not woken up.

"I did try to wake you up," the woman told her cousin. "I knew I was awake because I was talking to you."

Her mother was getting very concerned and wanted to send the woman to a psychiatrist. Her mother thought she was breaking down over the loss of her grandmother. It was the first time that she had lost someone close to her. Her mother wanted her to go see someone, so she knew her daughter would be getting some help if she needed it. Her mother had found her a psychiatrist because her daughter's grief was so strong, and now she was very worried about how her daughter was talking about these ghosts.

The woman herself didn't really feel it was necessary to send her to a psychiatrist. Yet she was also wondering whether these other people were right. Was she just really going crazy? She had been hoping and wishing her grandmother would really be here. Yet the negative questioning she received from other people made her doubt it was possible. Her grandmother's death, the ghosts, and the way people in her life responded to her experiences really bothered her. She was getting really worked up about it all. And she didn't know how long this (seeing the ghosts) was going to keep happening. Was she going to go through this for months? She just didn't know.

These ghostly apparitions were just very eerie. The thing that most made them eerie for her was the way she woke up. It just was, like, boom! Again, it wasn't that she'd had a bad dream. It wasn't that she heard a noise. It was just that she had woken up out of a sound sleep. She had never felt afraid of the ghosts. She had never felt any fear, never felt that they would hurt her. She had been a little surprised by the first one she saw, because she had never seen anything like these ghosts before. But they never made her feel uncomfortable. She had never really even been given information on the dark silhouettes that she saw. She perceived silhouettes or smoke or something there, but the outline of the person was very physical.

She remembered getting all worked up because now her family had gotten all worked up. They wanted to send her to a doctor, put her on medication, and all this other stuff.

One night as she was lying in bed, she was so upset, and she said out loud, "Okay, look, I believe my grandmother now. I really do. But please don't come and see me anymore. I believe it. I don't want to see you guys anymore. I don't want anything to do with this anymore because now my life is getting out of control." After that, she never saw the ghosts again.

Years later, her uncle was trying to find information about their family tree. Her family was from a small town in northern New Hampshire, where her grandfather had a general store. All their family had grown up there. She and her uncle had gone over to the town hall in this town, looking for records. There, they were looking at "all these pictures." Two of the people she thought she had seen as ghosts—the heavyset farmer and the older lady—were in those pictures. She didn't know whether they were relatives of hers, but they were exactly the same people she had seen. The older lady with the bun, in the shirt and dress, was in the pictures, very severe looking, and the heavyset guy with the farmer's jeans and the hat was there also.

She didn't see the third ghost, the young woman with the long hair, in any picture. Maybe the apparitions she had seen were relatives, she thought to herself.

"Maybe when you die, you need to wait for certain unknown influences or, like, a whole generation before you can come back," she said to her mother. "Maybe these are the older generations that are coming to say, 'Hey, your grandmother was right, but we don't want you to think that she's not thinking of you.'"

Side note: One might ask whether the younger woman this individual saw may have been her grandmother but how her grandmother looked at a younger age. If she had never seen her grandmother or pictures of her when the latter was younger, is it not possible her grandmother could appear to her to be a young stranger instead of the beloved grandmother she knew?

We will finish this chapter with a case of supernatural communication between sisters. The woman who shared it was a fifty-four-year-old married female. She worked as a quality assurance technician, was of Catholic faith, and had a two-year college degree.

Her sister, Mary, had been diagnosed with stage-4 cancer, and they knew she was not going to live much longer. Mary wanted to live with her while she was dying, and she did, for about eight months, before passing away in this woman's home. They were part of a very close family, and they had a support group helping take care of Mary. But she was the only family member there with Mary when she died. And after Mary died, her house went back to the way it was; she lived there by herself again.

At the time this woman worked for a local pharmacy. One day at work, she was in the back of the store and heard somebody calling her name. She ignored it until she heard her name called again. Then she went to the front of this store and asked if somebody needed her. Her coworkers said no. So she went back to what she was doing. She could have sworn somebody had talked to her, spoken her name.

A couple days later, she was in the back of this store by herself again and again heard her name being called. She went to the front of the store and asked who needed her. Again, nobody did. So she walked to the back and heard her name called again. This pattern happened again several different times in the course of a couple months.

One night she came home and was getting ready to go to bed. She went up the stairs to her bedroom and heard her name being called. It sounded like her sister's voice, which made her think she was probably just missing her sister. She hadn't cried much when her sister died, only at the funeral. Her sister had lived with her almost a year. She thought maybe she hadn't let her sister's death go yet.

She heard her name called a couple more times, and she began to think she might be going out of her mind. When she had first heard her name called, she was kind of thrown, but because it happened at work, she kept thinking someone else in the store was calling her. In her house, it could only have been her sister. The voice sounded like her sister's, too. She thought she was cracking up or having a mental breakdown. Maybe she was missing her sister and had some mental issues going on. She called and spoke to her doctor, who said her mind was helping her heal.

She began internally talking to her sister: "Well, I was telling you I was hearing your voice, and I heard your voice again at work." One night she came home and was in bed, across the hall from the room where her sister had once slept. Again she could hear her sister saying her name. She asked, "Is that you?" and heard, "Ha, ha," and her name again.

On another night she was on her way up the stairs and heard her name called again. The room where her sister had stayed toward the end of her life was back down on the first floor. The woman stopped and asked if the invisible person calling her name was her sister. In response, she just heard her name again.

"I am okay," she said to the voice. "You can go now. You can leave me. I'll be okay." After she said those words, she never heard her name called again.

She thought that before she had heard her sister's voice, she hadn't been ready to let her sister go. Her sister living with her, she guessed, had created a greater attachment between them than she'd thought. After she said, "You can let me go," her sister had let her go.

Her sister was always one to say, "I am going to come back. I'm going to find you a man. I'm going to take care of you. You wait and see. I'm going to come back." And you know, she thought her sister *was* coming back. Even though she was the kind of person who liked closure, she didn't want closure at the time because there had been so much death in her family already. Her sister's death had been devastating for the whole family. Her sister had lived with her the whole time she was sick, which was almost a year, and she hadn't wanted to see her sister go.

Years before this happened, when she was probably sixteen years old, her grandmother had told her about an unusual experience she'd had. Her grandmother was a very sane woman, a very sharp and smart woman, a businesswoman, and not a hallucinator or anything. But her grandmother said she had woken up one night, sat up in bed, and saw her dead husband at the bottom of her bed. Her husband came and sat on the bed, put his face in his hands, looked up at her, and said her name.

Her grandmother said she pinched herself to see if she was wake, and she was. He looked at her and shook his head, saying, "No." He called her name and said, "Oh, oh, oh!" Then he disappeared. Her grandmother said she felt like her husband had come to tell her that something was going to happen.

At the end of that week, her cousin was killed in a farming accident. Because of the visit from her dead husband, her grandmother was already prepared.

Her grandmother had said she didn't think anybody would have believed her story: "Nobody would have believed that I saw your grandfather." But she did tell her sister-in-law the next day what had happened. This sister-in-law thought her grandmother, who was in her sixties, was insane, cracking up, or having a mental breakdown. Yet the rest of her family all believed her.

Her grandmother said that her grandfather had come to her to let her know that she would be strong enough to get through what it was that was going to happen (her cousin's death). Her grandmother was always a strong woman in their family. She thought her husband thought this death would be too much for her, but she said she knew something was going to happen. Based on her grandmother's experience, this woman now thought her sister, Mary, had come to tell her that she was strong enough to go on without her.

In many cases of after-death communication, there seems to be evidence that is only for the individual having the experience; such evidence is not able to be replicated by others, and it is not necessary that others replicate it. For example, I communicated with a thirty-eight-year-old, divorced registered nurse. She was of Italian descent and had a bachelor's degree in nursing. She told me about the murder case of her sister, who was shot and left on the side of the road in the snow in upstate New York.

This nurse described her experience as an out-of-body experience and a dreamlike state. Her sister had come to her and communicated that the authorities had caught her murderer, but he would get off on a technicality because crucial evidence, found in his trunk, had been discovered without a search warrant. Shortly after, her father called and told her everything had happened just the way her deceased sister had told her.

Later her dead sister visited her again, this time to take her to a gathering to meet some friends. There were several famous musicians and actors at the ghostly gathering—people she did not realize her sister knew or had known. (The spirit of) one musician said to her, "You are not supposed to be here. You are still alive." Then she saw a famous actor who, to her knowledge, was still living. She said to him what the musician had said to her: "You are not supposed to be here either. You are still alive." He informed her that his girlfriend had murdered him, saying, "It wasn't an accident. She did it on purpose." Her sister had brought her to this ghostly gathering to prove to her that she (her sister) still existed after death.

Afterward, she told her father what she had experienced. He said, "Well, he (the actor) is still alive, so I guess that wasn't true." She feared he thought she was insane for saying such things. The following evening, it was announced on television that this actor had died of an overdose.

These examples demonstrate that something is going beyond what we can know through the common, everyday ways we attain knowledge. In all of these cases, such events provided sufficient evidence for the experiencer that their loved ones continued to exist in some manner after death. This would be another example of subjective truth. Those who had these experiences didn't know how they gained this information, but such experiences suggest there is something greater than we can comprehend going on around us.

The case of the clinical director earlier in the chapter presents us with information and an experience that suggest there is more happening in our universe. She was able to perceive changes in her environment that suggested a shift in her awareness. She experienced the beings she encountered as external to herself and what she considered to be her essence of life. She also experienced them as present *within* her at moments. She sensed an opening up and a closing down at the same time. For her, these experiences were all she needed to be sure there is more to existence.

The case of the accountant who saw spirits after her grandmother died presents a typical mixture of perceptual responses from others advocating for their point of view. Such responses are often a characteristic of supernatural movies where the hero is misunderstood by the people who cannot think out of the box. This individual's case was also an out-of-the-blue experience (see Chapter 2), and she felt like she was losing her mind (see Chapter 4) since her prior reality had not included such characteristics of the universe. Her story demonstrates how those who have supernatural experiences often struggle when other people don't accept those experiences as real. In her case, receiving validation from her fiancé and from the pictures at the town hall helped her feel supported.

When she talked to these ghosts or spirits, these occurrences stopped. Other people I have spoken to in my research experienced the same thing. I have experienced it myself. At one point in my life, two people I knew died in the same week. The first was a friend who had recently had a second heart transplant, but her body rejected the new donor heart. The second person was a client I had worked with in the past. Before they died, I'd had engaged with each of them in lengthy discussions about life after death. Soon after their deaths, I would turn off the lights, and the lights would come back on. I would turn off the television, and the television would come back on. I explained away these occurrences as an electrical problem, even though I never had such problems in my house the whole time I had lived there. Next, very strangely, the CD player in my car began to open and close of its own accord while I was driving. This had never happened before. At that moment I said, "I don't know which person you are, but I get it. You still exist. I understand." No more odd occurrences happened with the lights, television, or CD player after I made that statement.

Such interactions and their meanings are usually really personal and subjective. They don't mean anything to someone else but are very meaningful to the person experiencing them. We need to not ignore these interactions.

How can we overcome the restrictions on our consciousness? How can we expand our awareness beyond others' perceptual limitations? By finding new meanings and perceptual possibilities in our everyday life experiences.

Reflections: There seems to be a level of communication that occurs between us and our deceased loved ones. While after-death communication is by no means commonplace, it happens more frequently than has been acknowledged or reported.

When someone experiences communication with a deceased loved one, they also often receive information validating the experience, and that validation helps them go on. If you have such an experience, you may be able to find peace within by sending love to those who have passed on, which can help you and them heal in ways you cannot even begin to understand immediately. You can often find a sense of harmony if you remember your past experiences with those you love, and know you were blessed to spend time with them, to learn from them, and to grow together with them. In more difficult moments, they are hard lessons that help define you.

Exercise: If a loved one reaches out to communicate with you after their death, ask yourself the following questions:

1. When this person appeared, was there any significance to what was going on at the moment? Was there a connection between that person's appearance and something else in your life?
2. Did this person provide you with any information that only mattered to you? Or did you receive information that realistically validated some circumstance or event in your life?
3. How did this experience affect your views on life after death? Did this experience show you that your supernatural awareness reaches out beyond the perceptual limitations you have learned or been taught?

Part III

Protecting Your Supernatural Awareness

This final section is about what takes place within you as you begin to open to a new reality and recognize there are more influences in the world and universe than you thought there were. You have come to accept your supernatural experience and perhaps are actively seeking to have others.

First, we will examine the need to use our supernatural awareness responsibly and the need for protection from potentially harmful supernatural forces. Then I will summarize twelve key findings from my extensive research on supernatural experiences and individuals who have them. If you are interested in developing (or further developing) your supernatural awareness, these findings may well prove to be useful and encouraging. Lastly, we return to the subject of protection, this time addressing the need to protect yourself from skeptics, who take great pleasure in disproving and disbelieving the supernatural sphere. Because they usually haven't had any supernatural experiences themselves, they typically seek to defend the world as they have experienced it while denying there are any other possible parts to the universe.

Chapter 9

Ethical Supernatural Awareness: Using Your Gifts Responsibly

I remember a man who told me he was very uncomfortable around a spiritual woman whom he felt wanted more from him than he was willing to share. After seeing her one night, he went home at 3:00 a.m. and did a meditation/self-hypnosis session in which he put a bubble of white light of protection around himself and imagined severing a cord that connected him to this woman. At 3:30 a.m., she called him, wailing and crying and unable to talk. Although this man spoke with her on several more occasions, he understood her call as validation that he needed to severe this friendship because it was unhealthy for him.

Just because someone develops supernatural awareness doesn't mean they will use that awareness in an ethical way. Sometimes our human imperfections create difficulties with our expanding supernatural awareness. In this chapter, I will outline some of the pitfalls that can happen to people when they enter the realm of awakening consciousness, seek advancement, or gain supernatural abilities. An individual who is well meaning and in good relationship with others brings a sense of balance and harmony into all their interactions in all spheres of living—not just the physical, mental, and emotional spheres, but also the supernatural sphere. An individual who is not well meaning and in good relationship with others will bring just the opposite: imbalance, discord, and potentially harm.

I present several examples of supernatural awareness gone awry. The first three cases center on individuals who are misusing their supernatural awareness in some form. The fourth case demonstrates how consuming drugs or alcohol can open people to negative supernatural influences.

This first case comes from a forty-five-year-old married male of Hungarian ancestry who had two years of college. In his interview, he noted that he had received marital counseling in the past, had back pain, and did not have any substance abuse problems. The development of his supernatural awareness had given him a number of extraordinary abilities, such as the ability for part of him to leave his physical body and travel to different places (astral travel), the ability to move objects with his mind (telekinesis), and the ability to sense supernatural beings like ghosts. He also revealed that he could take energy from others when they weren't protecting themselves, without them being aware of it.

It was in the last five years to eight years that he started to learn about astral travel. When he discovered that he had an ability to astral travel, he started reading about out-of-body experiences on the Internet. Once in a while, he would get a book about the topic from a library, but most of his reading he would do online.

He learned how to refine his ability by developing a process of meditating and getting himself ready for astral travel when he went to sleep at night. This preparation consisted of getting his concentration and his mind set for leaving his body, as well as just "getting settled down" and relaxed for meditation. He looked forward to the traveling. Sometimes he ended up going someplace surprising, not where he wanted to go. He was always excited; for him, astral travel was like getting in his car to go for a drive in the country.

Once in a rare while, when he was at work, no one bothered him, and it was nice and quiet, he could make a quick trip for a few minutes. But most of the time, he would travel at night when he went to bed and was preparing to go to sleep. He would start right away with his meditation and his deep-breathing exercises. He would settle himself down and completely relax. He emptied his mind of all thoughts, all memories, and all feelings. He thought about just one thing, relaxing, and did not jumble his mind with daily thoughts.

All these things he'd read talked about a silver thread that keeps the astral body connected to the physical body. But he had never had a silver cord or thread. Instead, for him, the physical body had some kind of physical homing device. He always found his way back into his body. He had his own way of leaving his body: he envisioned himself standing up and starting to walk on invisible stairs, stepping up higher and higher and higher, while thinking of the place he wanted to go. Sometimes a location was here on Earth, but sometimes places he traveled were not on this earth.

He used to do a lot of chatting with people on the Internet. He met this woman in Salem, Massachusetts—a very nice lady, about the same age as he was. She was a divorcee and had a child. He didn't know how, but as he was chatting online with her one day, he got onto the subject of astral travel, and she was okay with that subject. After she became interested in this ability, she said, "Why don't you come and visit me?"

He said, "I suppose I could try." (He noted that he didn't astral travel to visit people without their permission. He respected other people's privacy and limits to their personal space.)

So one night he actually did astral travel to this woman's home. He went to Salem in his dreams. He just stood there in her bedroom of her old Victorian house, looked around, and came back—just a quick trip. He perceived the colors purple, green, and velvet in her room—colors of her bedspread, her curtains, and her wallpaper. The next day, he described to her what her room and its furniture looked like. She told him she had actually felt him there. She had kind of seen a shimmering in the room at the time he said he'd been there.

He also described her lavender perfume, which he had smelled there. It was his first experience of being able to smell (something in the location he was visiting).

When he traveled, he couldn't really touch solid objects, but he could feel them. Everything has an energy, and he could feel energy of things. For instance, he was color blind to a certain extent, yet by touching an object, he could almost tell the object's color by its energy. As far as putting his hands on things or their energy, as far as feeling the difference between, say, furry and rough or hot and cold, he didn't use the same sense of touch that you'd use for physical objects. Instead, he can put his hand on an object, and a thought would come to his mind telling him what that object felt like or what color that object is. That's about as close as he could get to describing feeling things he couldn't touch. It was hard to explain.

After this Salem woman and he had chatted for a couple of years, visiting her became a regular thing. He visited her sometimes three times a week. These visits to the woman in Salem went on for a very, very long time. He never could prefect his landings. He kept crashing into her furniture. And then one time, he crashed while coming home to get back into his body. He crashed into a wall and knocked all the pictures off that wall. (Afterward, his wife asked him how those pictures had fallen off the wall. He still had the two picture frames that had broken when he returned to his body.)

He and this Salem woman had a mutual friend, Gretchen, up in Maine, and Gretchen had a dog. One time he astral traveled to visit Gretchen, and Gretchen's dog sensed him. The dog actually started going crazy, just barking, running around in circles, and chasing him away. The dog was yipping a lot. Up until that point, he'd had no idea that animals could sense his presence. He also had a friend in Alaska who had a cat, and when he astral traveled to visit that friend, her cat was not concerned about his presence appearing there. But Gretchen's dog was quite sensitive about his visiting. His friend in Salem had a dog too, and it did sense him. But this dog did nothing at all and didn't care about his appearing there. It was just Gretchen's dog who reacted negatively toward his presence. Gretchen's dog saw him. He could tell that this dog looked at him and really, truly sensed him. It wasn't just barking at the moon. This dog startled him. As fast as he had gotten there, he left. Afterward, Gretchen said, "Don't do that again." So he didn't go up there again.

Another time, he went to visit his friend in Alaska. He described to her the next day what she had looked like and how she was sitting, and according to her, what he described was pretty accurate.

At the time of our interview, he said he hadn't astral traveled to visit someone for probably a year. He didn't just go anyplace. He could see himself flying over the surface of the planet. Sometimes he went through the middle of the planet. It depended on whether he wanted to take the scenic route or the direct route.

This astral travel wore him out. He would be dead tired the next day. One of those trips took him about three days to recover fully from. He would sleep twelve hours at a time. This astral traveling really drained him. He remembered once sleeping through an entire weekend.

When he was traveling, he didn't feel temperatures or feel any differences in temperature.

He discovered that time takes on a different meaning when he was astral traveling. There was no time. He could go, now, and they (the people where he was going) wouldn't see his appearance, feel his presence, or know he visited, if he wanted. Sometimes he could control when his presence would appear at a different location in the physical time. He might appear at a location a couple of days later than when he actually astral traveled there, for example. He doesn't know how that worked.

He could go somewhere and come back, and the next day someone there would say, "You were just here."

"Oh no, that was yesterday," he'd tell them.

"Oh no, just now you were here," they'd reply.

This part of astral traveling was like playing hide and seek; leaving his body and appearing somewhere else was like revealing your hiding place when you felt like appearing and letting the other person find you. Altering when others saw him appear was about the only way he could describe it. Sometimes when he appeared was not really under his control. Or maybe he was just not aware of the process of appearing to others and their seeing him later. He felt sneaky about appearing; he didn't want others to see him. He felt this hiddenness, staying hidden, didn't always work that way. Appearing later didn't always work. Sometimes when he would try not to let others see him, they did anyway.

Whether he could delay his appearance while astral traveling depended on how much energy he had saved up and how much control he had over himself and his surroundings. He had to get enough sleep to refresh himself, or he had to find a source of energy or take energy from others to augment his own. In these moments, he ignored others' boundaries and took energy from people without their knowing. He acknowledged that I would not approve of these actions and said he viewed this situation as being others' fault, because they were not protecting themselves.

He had talked to somebody about taking energy from others just a few days before our interview. The other guy had said, "You are not supposed to do that. That's called psychic vampiring." Psychic vampires feed off the psychic energy and emotions of other living creatures, leaving their victims depleted and drained. This man would go into a crowd and feel everyone's energy. He would take a little energy from this person and a little energy from that other person. He had always thought it was okay to take energy from others, but the other guy had told him that taking energy from others was infringing on their rights and against the rules. He ignored the rules most of the time. He described himself as "a spoiled brat type of person." He could do what he wanted when he wanted to. He would worry about any consequences of his taking energy later.

A couple of days before he met with me, something really rather odd happened: there actually was something that came through his house. His wife woke up and shook him in their bed and said, "Did you hear that?" He was already awake and said, "Yeah, yeah, that ghost went scooting by. You could hear it, like, sitting in front of a stereo moving quickly from the right speaker to the left speaker." A couple of days later, his wife said she didn't remember any of that happening. He seemed to attract ghosts or spirits, and he had been getting himself consciously back into sensing them. He had all kinds of stuff coming through his house.

His friend in Salem had pointed out to him that since he had been going to see her, she'd been getting visited by many, many other different ghosts. She was like, "Why did you start coming here?"

Regarding the astral travel, it was easier for him to come back into his body than to go out of his body. The taking-off part— working up the energy, getting out there— was the hardest. He started to play around with that for a while, doing it deliberately. Sometimes it might take him two, three, four attempts to leave his body. Traveling out of his body felt like falling from high up somewhere. There was no jerking thud or anything like that when he tried to leave his body and fell back down. He thought that his ability to travel out of his body probably depended on his energy level. When he left and went out, he felt just as light as a feather. He never really paid attention to when he came back into his body, although one time he had a bruise from when he crashed into something on the way in. He actually got bruises from crashing into things.

He has been to "where the dead people are." They are none too happy about that; the dead didn't like people like him going there. He stopped going there, because teasing them wasn't nice. After all, he could leave and they couldn't. He remembered their sadness and anger. He remembered being told to leave, and he didn't want to leave. He could go there if he wanted to because he could. There are rules, and though he bent rules sometimes, he didn't break them. It was hard to leave the place of the dead the first time. There were some strong forces there that tried to drain his energy away. He probably went there about four or five times. Eventually, he thought, he got bored of going there, so he never went back.

He got bored of these things (his supernatural abilities) quickly too. He would find out he could do these things, and then he would think, "Okay, what's next."

He hadn't moved objects with his mind since 1985. Back in the early to mid-eighties, he and his wife became interested in pyramids. So they found a book that had directions on how to build a pyramid with the right dimensions and the right angles. He built some in different sizes out of cardboard and wood. He put these pyramids under his bed and on their coffee table. He hung these pyramids from his ceiling with strings, all over the house. And one of the things (he built) was this funky-looking thing—lots of pyramids on a circle, hung on string on the house. He could make it twirl left and right and swing back and forth. He thought that was the coolest thing.

He once put a piece of Styrofoam with a paper clip on it in a plate of water, and he could make it go all over the place. But that was draining. Making an object move just drained him.

He used to be able to make his closet door and his bedroom door open (without touching them). He could budge these doors a bit, a few inches here or there. There was a ghost that kept messing with his door. This ghost would open this door; this ghost would close this door. He would open this door; he would close this door. The man telling the story would open this door, being mean to the ghost, and then he would turn the light on and off in the closet.

He actually tried to focus a beam of energy, like Superman focusing his X-ray vision, with a beam coming out of his eyes. (Of course, there was this third eye thing up here on your forehead, he noted.) He would envision this energy there, much like the tractor beam coming off the starship *Enterprise* (from the TV show *Star Trek*). He would just say to himself, "Okay, put all this energy up there and send it out through your body. Focus it down onto this object, whatever it is, and place your eyes to where you want it to be. Then go back, look at the object. Look where you want it to be, look at the object, look where you want it to be, in rapid succession, until you feel it start to move toward that space. Once it starts to move, you can actually feel yourself connected to the object. All it takes after that is one little budge, and it keeps going, back and forth, round and round, spinning." He had been able to do that in his teenage years. He hadn't been able to move objects this way since then.

This individual's experiences demonstrate how someone can develop supernatural awareness and abilities on their own and what can happen when they do not develop ethics along with their awareness. When he took energy from others, he was utilizing what he had experienced in the only way he knew how at the time. This case demonstrates a need for us to be aware of supernatural phenomena and beings and to protect ourselves from such invisible influences, which are not always safe or well intentioned.

The person who shared the next story was a forty-two-year-old, Caucasian single mother, who was a Spiritualist and had a master's degree in psychology. She operated her own holistic business, teaching meditation, hypnosis, and Reiki, and conducting one-on-one healing sessions. She had an ability to perceive and interact with discarnate spirits.

She had gone to a house in New England that was known for being haunted. This house was a beautiful, giant yellow house built during the 1700s. This guy had bought it and was going to renovate and live in it. But this house turned out to be haunted. So, apparently, he had decided he was not going to live in that house. Instead, he gave ghost tours and charged fifty dollars a person for people to experience ghosts in that house. This woman disagreed with his choice, and was skeptical and indifferent about visiting the house. She didn't particularly like these types of haunted-house tours because she thought that people were exploiting the dead. However, when her girlfriend had the idea to go to this haunted house, she'd acted as if she were accepting or tolerant of this haunting situation, so as not to hurt her friend's feelings or this owner's feelings or make them feel bad.

When she and her friend arrived at this house, it was still daylight. They went in through a front door. The way that house was set up, there was a little mini hallway that led into a (larger) hallway, and on the right, was some kind of a room. It was hard to really judge what that room was because nothing was furnished. But on the right side there were these folding chairs that you could go and sit down in and wait for everybody to show up. So visitors paid for their fifty-dollar ticket, went into the house, and sat in this room (while waiting for the rest of the people who would be in the tour group). There was also a basement, a first floor, a second floor, and she believed, an attic. The house was kind of square based and had large rooms. All the rooms were kind of connected because this house was old.

In the waiting room, there was a white feather on the floor. Seeing it, she was like, "No reason for a white feather to be on the floor." She picked it up and showed it to her friend. She was like, "This is a sign here. You know this." For her, finding or receiving a white feather had meaning. Another time, she had gone to buy a car new. She was looking at some cars at a car lot and had a few to choose from. One car she saw had a white feather on a wheel. She had seen that feather and picked it up. She remembered showing this feather to her daughter. She had bought the car that had had the white feather on it; it was the car she currently had (at the time of the interview). White feathers for her are angels saying, "Pay attention here."

There had been no reason for there to be a white feather on that car, but even so, seeing that feather had been more likely than finding a white feather in this guy's house.

Then, in her head, a little boy ghost showed up. This little boy ghost came up to her, and in her head, she was like, "What are you doing?"

"Are you here to do a walk-around thing?" he asked.

"Yep," she said.

"Hah, okay," he said. He appeared kind of annoyed.

Then some physical people came into this room, sat down, and talked. They said, "We're going to break you up into groups. We're going to explain the history of this house and all the stuff and what went on." There were eight visitors and two tour guides. The guy who owned that house came out and talked about events that he understood to be examples of haunting. These stories set the stage for the guests to seek out new ghost experiences in this house. This owner presented an opportunity for people to experience a ghost for themselves.

"Now we're going to break into groups," he told the visitors. "Some of you are going to go with this tour guide. Others are going to go with that other tour guide. You're going to go through several parts of the house and just kind of roam around. Then they're going to talk and do their little spirit box thing." (A spirit box is an electronic device in which ghosts apparently use radio frequencies to communicate with the living. The ghosts grab a word or phrase that they hear as they scan through various channels.) He said they were going to do an EVP recording. (Electronic voice phenomena, or EVP, are voices thought to be those of spirits, of beings from another dimension. The phenomena are heard in researchers' own voices, in coincidental noises in the environment from unknown sources, or in the white noise of things like a radio station white noise or other electronic media.) The owner added, "You're going to do little meditation things. You're going to do all sorts of stuff."

All the lights in this house were off, and that was a creepy thing. She also totally disagreed with this process. She was like, "This sucks because this is exploiting the dead." Her friend strongly opposed anything that contradicted her view that this tour was favorable because she wanted to see evidence of a ghost presence.

As this woman moved around that house with the other guests and the tour guides, the little boy ghost kept following her. The first thing the visitors looked at was the room that was off to the left of the front door, where she and her friend had first come in. There was a ghost lady in that room. This ghost lady was pretty angry and, the woman said, "came at me really hard in my head." She couldn't really see what the ghost lady looked like. She knew it was a lady and that this lady had "one of those bonnet kind of a things" on her head. The ghost lady came flying at her in kind of a blur. The woman, seeing this ghost setting a boundary, backed up. The ghost lady pushed her back. So she knew this house was indeed haunted.

Next, she and the other guests had followed the tour guide upstairs into a room she guessed was a bedroom. In that room were all these folding chairs in a circle. The guests were all going to sit there and meditate with a tour guide. Meditation was how she already communicated with ghosts, and so she thought, "This is ridiculous." But she sat down and entered into her meditation while everybody was sitting there.

The little boy ghost had come into her mind while she was meditating. "Now I can talk to him more," she thought.

"What are you doing?" she asked him.

"How many times is this going to happen?" he asked.

"How often does this happen?"

"All the time."

"How many of you are here?" the woman said. "Bring them all in here."

So this ghost child brought other ghosts, and she could see all these dead people, kind of like expressing dissatisfaction: "We're so sick of this. This is getting old."

"Are you stuck here?" And they are like, "Yeah, we're stuck."

"Tell you what," she said. "I'm going to let you go. I'm going to bring down these stairs that go up to an entryway to the next world. And you're going to go up these stairs and move along and do your thing, and you'll be unstuck."

She brought down the stairs. The ghosts all moved on.

The ghost child said, "Oh my God, thank you!"

"Go, go," she told him. "I'm running out of time. Go!" And so he ran. She shut the door behind him.

When the tour guides were like, "Okay, we're going to end the meditation," she was like, "Okay, cool."

Next the tour guides said, "We are going into the next room, and we're going to do a little EVP ghost box thing—that thing that sounds like a static radio thing." But then nothing came through. Nothing.

"This is weird," the tour guides said. One guide who had done this tour multiple times said, "This doesn't make sense. Nothing is coming through. I don't get it."

The guests went to the next room, and the same thing happened. The tour guide said, "We're going to do this thing," but then nothing happened.

At that point, this woman's friend said to her, "What did you do?" And she was like, "It's fine."

The guests kept going around from place to place, but nothing would happen. The tour guide kept saying, "I don't understand this. How can nothing be happening?"

Finally, the tour guides said, "So we are ready to take a break." At this point, it was dark. They all went back downstairs where the hosts had set up a table with doughnuts.

As she and her friend were sitting there, her friend said, "What did you do?"

"They were trapped here, being used like zoo animals, treated like some kind of tourist attraction, and they are people," she told her.

"You couldn't have let them go after the tour?" her friend demanded. "We paid fifty bucks each to get in here."

"I get your point. I get that. Sorry," she said.

Another tour group had been in a different section of the house. The two groups met up at a crossing point in the tour, and the group leaders of their group asked the leader of the other group, "Are you getting anything?"

"No, we're not getting anything," the other group leader said. And they're like, "How is that even possible?"

Then the owner came in and said, "What do you mean, you're not getting anything? You are always getting stuff here."

"We know," the group leaders said. "But we're not getting anything."

They began asking all the people on the tour, "Have you felt anything?"

"No," the guests said.

"Have you seen anything?"

"No."

"I don't understand," the owner said. "That never happens. What do you mean?"

In her head, the woman thought, "Well, you know what? It serves you right. They (the ghosts) are not pets."

Finally, the tour guides for her group said, "Okay, we're going to go downstairs to the basement." The other group went upstairs. When she and the guests she was with entered the basement, there was some kind of like a vortex, some kind of a door, down there. (A paranormal vortex is a location in space or an energy spot where ghosts can travel between this world and the next world.) Again, the guides are like, "We're going to meditate."

"Great," the woman thought. "We're going to seal this (vortex) off, because that's kind of how these things are getting through in the first place. Seal this off." She could feel something coming at her. This thing was animalistic. It was human, but it had kind of been there a while. She was like, "Dude, I'm going to let you go, but you got to kind of calm down."

So she shut down the vortex.

"We're getting nothing down here," said the tour guides. "No EVPs. No ghost box thing. No nothing."

Finally, both tour groups and their guides came together at the end of the tour. "We're really sorry," they told the guests. "This really didn't go right. This doesn't happen. We don't know why."

The woman silently said to herself, "Yeah, they're not pets, but whatever."

So she and her friend left.

"What did you do?" her friend asked again.

"I let them go."

"You couldn't have let them go after?" Her friend had wanted to experience a ghost presence. "Why did you let them go? We each paid fifty dollars, so one hundred dollars, to walk into that thing."

"They're not pets. These are people that are stuck, they are being exploited."

To that, her friend replied with a sigh.

She went back home and meditated. She talked to her spirit guides and asked, "Is their house empty? Are you going to be able to keep them away?"

Her spirit guides said, "They're just going to call them back—not these same ghosts, new ghosts. They are just going to keep calling them back because that's what they do." Her guides told her the owner and tour operators were thinking, "We are going to do a little séance, and we are going to call them all in." They would be just calling new ghosts. She had cleaned this house out, and they had been like, "What you mean nothing is happening?" They were kind of panicking because there were eight people who had paid their fifty dollars and weren't getting anything. This owner was saying, "That never happens." He panicked a little bit over it. She had thought that this guy was stupid. He shouldn't be exploiting the dead anyway, so (losing his ghost tours) served him right.

She believed this owner was more concerned about his finances than about gaining knowledge or helping others. He had been talking about selling that house, but he wasn't going to. About a month before she and her friend had been there, he'd had a television show crew come to the house and acquire all kinds of evidence of hauntings. The show had aired an episode about that house, where viewers could see all that evidence that the crew was collecting. She thought this owner had been on a couple television shows. They had physical evidence that the house was haunted.

Yet she had emptied that house of ghosts. "Sorry, guy, but this is how I feel about that," she imagined telling the owner.

In running his ghost tours, the owner *was* demonstrating that there are ghosts and giving people an idea that they may exist beyond this life. But he didn't think past that phenomenon. This woman verified, in her inner subjective experience, that the ghosts in this house existed. Then she also took another step: she helped them rather than just experiencing them and letting them be. She, her friend, and the owner of the house all perceived this haunted-house situation differently. These differences were analogous to those in many situations of everyday life: in some situations, some people are spectators, witnessing what happens; other people are the doers, creating the circumstances; and other people are problem-solvers, coming along and helping rectify the problems the situation reveals. Every individual progresses in their personal growth at their own pace, and which type of person they are in a given situation depends on what they need to achieve at that time.

When we have a skill or a gift, I believe we need to use it to help others and make the world a better place. Helping others meet their own needs and grow gives them an incredible gift of freedom. However, some people have difficulty meeting their own needs and can't see beyond these needs and desires. Worse yet are those that are just very selfish and have difficulty ever putting others before themselves. The following case gives us an example of someone who seemed to have genuine supernatural power, yet made no real effort to enhance the lives of others with it. Instead, he sought to use his power to control others for his own ends.

The person who shared this account was a seventy-five-year-old, American, divorced male of Scandinavian descent. He had a master's degree and was of Christian faith. He had always been very open to exploring supernatural knowledge.

He was living in Milford, New Hampshire, in a studio apartment. For some job-related reason, he had occasion to go to the Nashua, New Hampshire, post office on a regular basis. One day when he went to that post office, he saw a blonde-haired young man named Robert in the box section. He noticed Robert had several books on psychic phenomena, UFOs, and things of that nature. This material consisted mostly of books, some pamphlets, recordings, and recorded programs on videotape—

not things he'd made but things that he had purchased. He was mailing these materials out.

The man had seen Robert there several times. On that day, he began talking to Robert and asked what he was doing with those books, as he was interested in such things. Robert said, "We have a correspondence course." He was mailing these lessons out. "If you're interested, we have little meetings once in a while," Robert told him. He took Robert's telephone number and didn't think about it any further.

The man used to attend psychic events and belonged to a UFO group and another couple of social groups of that nature. There was a group called the Psychic Research Society of New Hampshire and Massachusetts, headed by a fellow named Norm Gauthier. Norm was a former radio host and ghost hunter in Manchester, New Hampshire, back in the day. Norm was interested in supernatural subjects. He used to be on the radio on Halloween, and others from all over country would interview him on TV and radio. Norm created this Psychic Research Society, and he would have guest speakers. The man had been one of those guest speakers, having spoken a couple times on ancient civilizations and dreams. Through that group, he knew a woman named Cindy, who was also interested in supernatural phenomena. Soon after talking with Robert at the post office, he ran into her and told her what Robert had said.

Cindy said, "You know, I know them. I ran into them too. They want me to come over, but I'm afraid to go over there alone. Will you go with me?"

"Yeah, I'll go with you," he said.

So she made the arrangements, and they went to this house. There were three other people there. There was Robert, who was maybe twenty-four years old and an easygoing person. There was a woman named Ashley, who was in her thirties, and there was another guy, named Cypher. This man and Cindy came in and sat down. Cypher, Robert, and Ashley were very cordial.

He said, "What do you do?"

Cypher said, "I have this school." He took the two of them down to the basement, where he had bookshelves and all these books on "psychic stuff, anything to do with any of the paranormal."

"We have this course," Cypher said.

"What do you teach?"

"We teach witchcraft," he said. "We have students all over the world—for example, in Australia. We take these books, loan them, and send them out. Students pay for the course, read the book, and send them back. We send them tests and have them do exercises and stuff like that."

The man said, "Oh, that is interesting. How did you learn all this?"

Cypher said, "We had this idea. It is a good idea."

They and Cypher finally went back upstairs. As they were all sitting around talking, the man noticed that Robert seemed to be very intimidated or controlled by Cypher and was very subservient to him. Robert would do tasks such as picking up the mail, going to the post office on his bicycle, and doing the grocery shopping. Robert was Cypher's errand boy. Cypher would instruct Robert to go to the store and send him to do all his chores. Cypher would sit around and psychically have his way with Robert. Cypher told the man, "He's a good, obedient guy. He would never harm anyone." According to the man, Robert was under a heavy influence of Cypher, who was guiding his every move. Robert was like a servant; he was doing his bidding and didn't get much in return.

This man thought that Cypher could use his mental and emotional energy to affect the physical world. Ashley seemed to be very tense and looked a little rough around the edges. By "a little rough around the edges," he didn't mean that Ashley looked rough in her demeanor or in how she spoke. He meant that she looked beat up. She looked like she'd "been through the mill," abused, haggled, worn down, had rough times. She looked aged and very stressed. Physically there was something about her, like someone had beat her up. When Cypher would talk, Ashley would chime in, "Oh yeah, and we would do this and do that." Cypher had this grin as if to say, "You're being a good girl, behaving now, and if you get out of line..." In fact, Cypher more or less said something during that conversation intimating that if Ashley didn't do as she was told, she knew what Cypher would do. The man didn't think Ashley was treated well. He thought Cypher had an ability to bruise Ashley or make her feel physical pain without touching her. Even though Cypher said, "I love her, though. She's my girl," he was controlling Ashley. He felt Cypher thought he could control women psychically. At times during the conversation, Ashley looked terrified.

Cypher said he had magically created things that appeared in the physical material world.

"That chair you're sitting in, I conjured that chair," Cypher said. "That chair never used to be here. I brought that chair into existence. Isn't that right, Ashley?"

"Ah yeah, that is right," Ashley said.

Cypher continued, "We needed a chair, and I conjured that chair." *Conjured* was the word Cypher used. Some people use the word *conjuring* metaphorically—as in, "Gee, I need another XYZ for my collection, or I'm trying to find a certain type of piece of furniture for my home, and I'm hoping I can finally run into it in the store or online or something." But when Cypher told them that he'd conjured the chair, he didn't mean he'd found it in a store or had someone give him one. He meant that he'd created it out of thin air—not instantaneously, but over time, the chair had manifested. They were being led to believe this guy created this chair out of nothing. Cypher had left that room, and when he came back, the chair was there.

Just then, a little black and white cat came by. Cypher said, "I conjured that cat too—not just now, but that is how we got the cat. I'm very good at doing conjuring things."

Then he added, "People do as I say. Isn't that right, Ashley?"

"Oh, yeah," she said.

Then Cypher proceeded to tell them, "I'm only renting here, but I would actually like to buy that house across the parking lot. I went over to talk to the woman (who owned the house)." Cypher said that he "projected to her." He claimed he had put the thought "You will sell me this house" in this female homeowner's mind, even though initially she would have nothing to do with selling her house.

"She is going to sell to me," Cypher said. "As a matter of fact, she came over and knocked on my door." Cypher said she had come over in a relatively short period of time, like a month or six weeks later after he had projected to her. She'd said, "Now I want to sell my house."

Cypher and the man talked back and forth. Cypher asked him a couple questions about UFOs, and the conversation was kind of cordial. But he was very explicit about who he was, saying he was very powerful and he could conjure up all this stuff. Throughout the conversation, Cindy didn't say anything. They spent maybe an hour, conversing back and forth.

The man said, "Nice mail order business." He had been in a mail-order business himself and talked to Cypher about that a little bit. "How do you get your customers?" he asked Cypher.

Cypher said, "I advertise in magazines, things of that nature. I'm self-taught. I'm really good at doing all of this. I know what I'm doing." What Cypher had meant was that he was really good at things such as conjuring and thought projections.

Eventually, the man said thank you for the information, and he and Cindy left very cordially, saying, "Nice meeting you."

Cindy came in her own car, so they drove away separately. Later, Cindy called him and said, "This guy is freaking creepy."

"Yeah, if he is really conjuring things and conjuring furniture," the man said.

"Do you really think he can do that? I think he did that."

"I believe him."

Cypher had said, "I conjured this cat from thin air. I conjured this chair. I did not go out and find one." And Ashley had said, "Oh, yes, he did. It is true." The man thought that Cypher had wanted a chair and couldn't find one. So he decided to conjure one, and he did. "Wouldn't you know now, the next time I came back in the room when I came home, there this chair was," Cypher had said. "I did the same thing with that cat, and I can do that again."

Cindy said, "I am not having anything to do with any of that."

She was frightened. She did not want anything to do with getting involved in something with Cypher. "I'm going to go home, and I'm going to say my prayers," she said. She was scared and didn't want Cypher trying to do anything to her, like projecting thoughts to her or messing with her head or bothering her or calling her. She didn't want anything to do with Cypher at all.

Cypher had wanted the man to mail him some information he had on UFOs. "You are going to mail that information," Cindy said to him.

"I'm going mail that information. I'm not going to put a return address on the mail, but I told him I was going to mail this information." He only mailed some sheets of paper—not a lot of material, not a booklet or anything. He did as he'd told Cindy he would: mailed this material on UFOs and didn't put any return address on the envelope.

Cindy also said, "I think he is roughing that woman up, if he doesn't get his way." She said that because Cypher had made some kind of innuendos indicating that if "this woman doesn't do" what he tells her to do, she suffers the consequences.

Cypher was into Ashley's mind, making her do what he wants her to do. Ashley didn't have any free will any more. Cypher was punishing her for any infraction. There was also the look Cypher had given her. During their conversation at the house, he had done all the talking, and Ashley had just reinforced what he'd said. Cypher would always give her a smirk or some kind of an expression that seemed to say, "You better say that," or "See, she's with me." There was just an attitude he had when he addressed her or looked at her. It was like Ashley was frightened to do anything. She was kind of stiff in a way, almost like she was being coerced in some way.

A month or so later, the man was in his apartment, a basement apartment that was the only studio apartment in the building. To come in, you first had to open the front door, and there was a foyer with a mailbox. Then you had to have a key to get through the next door. You needed to go down three or four steps, and then you came to a full apartment. Next you passed a laundry room, and then there was his studio apartment.

On this night, he was sleeping on his foldout sofa. It was the middle of the night, maybe two o'clock in the morning. He had been sleeping for a while. All of a sudden, he just woke up. He didn't think he physically woke up but mentally woke up. He remembered sitting up and coming out of his body. It wasn't a dream, but a dreamlike state. It wasn't like he floated above his house and looked down; it wasn't that type of out-of-body experience.

He sensed that Cypher was coming, and there was some danger. He could *see* this guy coming. He could see Cypher across the horizon, skipping or running across the roofs of houses. Cypher was standing up, without doing any motion. He was more or less leaning forward with his hands out. He was standing but bent over a little bit, leaning forward like he was running. But Cypher's legs weren't moving. Cypher wasn't flying, wasn't flapping his arms. He didn't have a cape, didn't have any of that stuff. He was just coming through the air from that direction of the man's home.

The man knew Cypher was coming to confront him somehow. He didn't know if Cypher was going to do something nasty to him or just make him aware that Cypher could get ahold of him anytime he wanted to find him. He knew Cypher was offended that he hadn't put his return address on the envelope he'd sent him. Cypher was going to prove to him that Cypher knew where he lived.

He pictured Cypher flying through the air, landing at the front door of his apartment building, and coming in the building. He knew Cypher was coming down the stairs and into his apartment. And if the man didn't stop him, he would be in trouble.

"He thinks he's going to come at me. I'll fix him," he thought.

Suddenly, he had a cross in his hand. He put his hand out, and a gold cross appeared there in his hand. It was approximately a foot long and nine inches wide. He knew this cross would protect him. The cross had these halos. It wasn't a Celtic cross that had a circle in the middle, but it had ball-type things on the ends of its points. The whole cross was gold and "was lit like crazy."

He then did the same thing Cypher had done and projected himself, like he was having an out-of-body experience. He just projected his essence right through his apartment door without opening it. He went out into that hallway and up the stairs.

When he first saw Cypher, he said, "You think you are going to come down to have your way with me. Well, I got news for you, because I got this cross. You are going to find out something that you don't know: that I have this power of protection."

He put the cross in Cypher's face. It wasn't just like he just showed Cypher the cross. He stuck this cross out at him. He actually shoved this cross in Cypher's face, so Cypher felt that cross of light. It was brightly lit, radiating and projecting a lot of gold light. He could hardly see because the halos were radiating light like crazy. The halos were very brilliant and had spikes of light. The spikes of light weren't all even; they were different lengths, almost like the spikes you see when someone spikes their hair. These spikes of gold light were coming out from 360 degrees around this cross and were very active.

He said to Cypher, "I will give you your medicine. I will fix you. I will take care of you."

Cypher was very frightened — terrified, in fact. This cross was radiating at him, and he recoiled from it. He instantly retreated, fled, was gone, left, disappeared. He just went right back the way he'd come — and quickly.

The man described the event as akin to someone breaking into your house. Instead of letting them take your stuff and leave, you confront them, bop them over the head, knock them unconscious, and call the police. It was like emergency action on his part, like quick draw at a gun fight. *I'll take care you. I'll show you who the real boss is. I'll show you who you're up against. You are not up against the average person. Someone here has a weapon or tool.* What happened was the opposite of what Cypher had hoped for. He had hoped to have frightened him, but Cypher was the one who ended up frightened.

He never heard a word from Cypher again, never heard any experience connected with Cypher again. This whole thing had happened in milliseconds. The experience was like a dream, yet it wasn't a dream but a dream-type state or almost like an out-of-body experience. It was like his life force had fought Cypher's life force.

Sometime after, the man asked Cindy, "Did you have anything happen to you?"

"No, I didn't have any problems," she said.

He told her what had happened to him. He said that Cypher had tried to come over and influence him or somehow do something to him or show him that "I am stronger than you" or something. He believed Cypher was trying to tell him, "I know where you live," because he purposely hadn't given Cypher his address. But, he told Cindy, "He won't be back anymore." He had given Cypher that cross in his face. So now he would not come around anymore. Cypher had probably never been defeated like that before or treated like that before. He had given Cypher a lesson.

He thought that Cypher really could do all the conjuring he had claimed and that he was up to no good. There was a strong undercurrent of arrogance because of his power. Cypher was evil, manipulated people, used people, influenced people. Cypher had an agenda that was not in anyone's best interest except his own. He wasn't doing anything positive but was up to mischief of some sort. He was worse than a bully. Cypher could suck your energy out and you wouldn't even know it. Cypher's was the classic sense of evil. He had no goodness in him; he didn't know or couldn't perceive goodness within him unless he could use such goodness to his advantage, to "buy you off or something." Cypher had no positives; it was all about him and what he wanted and how he could influence people, whatever his end was. This man was not alone in his thoughts about Cypher; Cindy had also thought Cypher was evil.

The man sensed that he was threatened by Cypher, and he took action. He was not frightened. He knew that he would win. At the same time, he did not want to pursue Cypher and have a confrontation. He just wanted Cypher to leave him alone. He figured if he went back and had a confrontation with Cypher, he may have come out bruised or not in a good way.

As our supernatural awareness develops, there is the potential that we could become vulnerable to harmful entities or nonphysical beings that can't be explained by the laws of nature as humans have defined them. I remember reading about a case presented in which an individual had either an out-of-body or near-death experience. In that disembodied state, he went to a bar and witnessed entities entering the bodies of very intoxicated individuals. You may remember from Chapter 6 the case in which a Brazilian woman with an expanded awareness described seeing a demon possess her alcoholic friend, Kate. It seems that some individuals, especially those with substance abuse issues, may be susceptible to such experiences as possession and discarnate spirits entering their inner being. There are a number of books written on this subject of possession. For example, in his book *Healing Lost Souls*, Dr. William Baldwin, a dentist with a doctorate in psychology, says that altering one's awareness with drugs or alcohol opens a door into your being for discarnate spirits.[9]

This next case was shared by a woman who had studied and had an interest in supernatural experiences all her life. She was sixty-six years old and of Irish and Danish descent. She had a two-year college degree. She was also an adult child of an alcoholic.

She was visiting her cousin in Phoenix, Arizona, around 1989 or 1990, during the summer. A bunch of people were sitting outside a small group of cabins. They were talking about supernatural things. Another cousin had just become a pilot and was talking about Area 51. Her cousin didn't know what was going on at Area 51, but he was interested in it because all pilots knew there were certain areas that they could not fly over, and Area 51 was one of those off-limits areas. All the people there that night were interested in talking about things like seeing ghosts.

Eventually, people started filtering out of the circle to retire for the night. She was left alone with this one blonde guy. She felt like she didn't have anything to fear from him because he was really skinny and very small in stature. He just did not look like he could be a threat to anybody. But she noticed that he had been drinking these really tall beers. She was amazed at how many of these beers he had drunk, but he was still sitting there and functioning.

She and this blonde guy continued talking about different types of metaphysical subjects. Suddenly, his head turned, and she saw this entity. It was the scariest thing she had ever seen in her life. That was saying something because throughout her life, she'd seen a lot of things that scared her. Growing up on a farm, she had seen animals getting hurt, for example. Some of the things she'd seen had really affected her. But this entity was beyond anything that she could even imagine. It emanated such dark, pure evil that she knew it was something she could not deal with alone.

She knew and just felt that this entity had actually taken over this blonde guy's body and his soul. She didn't know what that entity's intentions were, but she saw its potential for destructive acts that could cause injury, misfortune, or pain. She also didn't know if this evil entity was going to try and come out of that the other guy and come at her.

When she looked, it was like she was looking at this very black figure. She couldn't say that it had glowing red eyes, but it reminded her very much of the devil in (the 1940 Disney movie) *Fantasia*, in the sequence called "Night on Bald Mountain." Then she realized what she had been doing with her own body: She had crossed her legs in front of her body to protect herself. She was hugging her arms and hands to up near her throat to try and shield her torso.

She really felt so afraid that the entity was going to come out of this blonde guy and try to take her over. She didn't know what the rules are for entities trying or wanting to enter human bodies. She didn't know and still doesn't know if that entity could have just discarded the body of the blonde guy and taken over her body instead. She did not fear that this blonde guy would harm her physically because he just was so small, but she really felt so scared that somehow this evil was going to come at her and harm her in some way.

She knew and recognized "the dark" because of experiences she'd had in her life and in her childhood. When she saw or felt the dark, it was like a black cloud like in the (1990) movie *Ghost*, when the creatures come and take away the two guys responsible for murdering Sam Wheat.

She had been brought up Catholic, but she really had not been totally happy with the church and wanted to explore other things (other spiritual traditions). So she was trying other things, including witchcraft, but trying to remain away from anything dark. In witchcraft, she had not been able to find anything dark or associated with evil characteristics of witchcraft, at least with the people that she had dealt with. They had all seemed to be nature-loving just like her.

Given her experience with witchcraft, she called on the Goddess as she was sitting there, seeing the evil entity. She had been really trying to develop a relationship with the Goddess. Yet now she felt the Goddess was not going to be able to help her. She felt like she had no support whatsoever. She couldn't move and didn't know how she was going to get up out of her chair. She couldn't stand up and expose any part of herself, lest this evil come into her being.

Then this blonde guy had turned back to her, and she could no longer see the face of the evil directly. She could tell, though, that this evil was still there. When this blonde guy moved— really quick to the side, which for a drunk person seemed like it should have been impossible—that entity looked right at her. She could tell the guy was quite drunk and wasn't really focusing, but she could feel this entity was staring at her.

So she called on Archangel Michael. She had always heard that Archangel Michael would be able to combat evil. When she called on the archangel, she could feel energy, it came to the back of her. Archangel Michael was huge—six or seven feet tall and very, very sturdy and powerful. She immediately felt very safe. She asked him to put his wings around her body, and he did. She knew that whatever entity was sitting across from her was not going to be able to harm her.

She still didn't know how she ever finally managed to get up. She only knows that she knew she could safely move out of that situation. She was the only one sitting there with this drunk guy, and she knew that she could at least get into her cousin's cabin. As she was leaving, the evil entity spoke to her, in a voice that wasn't this blonde guy's.

"You will see me in the future," it said. "I'm not gone. You will face me in the future. Then I will get you."

Her cousin who had rented the cabin was off working because he worked nights. His brother, the pilot who had just finished flight school, had been watching TV and was just about ready to go to bed.

"We got to get out of here," she told him as she came into the cabin. She was frantic and panicked. "Jeff, you've got to get out of here. We've got to get out of here. You can get Kevin to move. He can't stay here. He's got to get out. There's evil out there."

She was going out of her mind trying to tell him what was happening. When her other cousin got home from work the next day, she told him, "You've got to move. You've got to get out of here. There's something evil in this area." She didn't remember if she told her cousins that the blonde guy had been taken over by an evil entity. She was not sure if she quite said that to her cousins, because at that point, she just was really babbling. She had never felt that strongly before or after about something that was that bad. She was aware enough to know the difference between a small threat and a bigger threat, and this entity experience was a big threat.

This final case demonstrates that we need to protect and care for ourselves at various levels, including being careful about what substances we take into our bodies. Of course, not everyone who is drunk is possessed or attached to a harmful entity, but stories like the previous one show what may happen when someone is in this situation. There are far more people denying possession is possible than there are people recognizing and treating such occurrences. One of the latter is Dr. Shakuntala Modi, a psychiatrist and author of the book *Remarkable Healings*.[10] In that book, she discusses attachments to harmful entities and offers a very detailed exercise for protection from external influences.

As you continue to develop your supernatural awareness, I strongly encourage you to not only protect yourself, but also protect others. To do so, you have to enhance your integrity, thoughtfulness, and social consciousness. When you do that, then what you do with your supernatural awareness will to bring a benefit to others.

Reflections: Remember that time and space are permeable. When using your supernatural awareness to interact with your universe, you need to be aware of and protect yourself from outside and inside influences that may create destructive occurrences. Recognize what surrounds you can enter into your inner being. Be vigilant of your own internal stirrings, knowing that they can reach out and impact another's internal or external environment. Recognize that what is invisible, such as psychic energy and inner thoughts and feelings, can manifest and connect to other living beings and things in ways that may not be beneficial to them.

Exercise: Experiment with these ideas:

1. Notice when you have unusual thoughts or images that are not common for you to experience. For example, if you enter a new space, such as a house that's for sale or the home of someone you don't know well, notice your feelings. Do you feel happy, sad, angry, heavy, or something else? Explore these feelings. You may find that there are sources outside of yourself that have evoked them.

2. Be aware of forces that take rather than give. Have you had any experiences in which you thought you may have encountered a person or force that sought to take something from you, such as your energy or life force?

3. Make sure you practice protecting yourself, especially when you think you might be around people or entities who are harmful, destructive, or selfish. Utilize a favorite method of self-protection, such as meditation, self-hypnosis, or prayer. Use this practice daily and notice if there are any changes in your day-to-day life or interactions with others.

An example of using protective imagery would be to envision a brilliant white bubble of light all around yourself. That bubble could be filled with florescent purple or green sparks that absorb, erase, or dissolve all negativity from your body, mind, emotions, and spirit. It could also function as a shield, deflecting all outside negativity, which bounces off it. There is a nice protection exercise in my first book, Perceptual Hypnosis, *that can also be helpful.*[11]

Chapter 10

Twelve Key Findings: Common Threads

As I began interviewing people about their supernatural experiences, one of my overarching questions was, what do these people and/or their experiences have in common? I believed that identifying the commonalities would help us better understand supernatural awareness. Although each person was unique, and each of their stories had distinctive details, over time, I began to see common patterns within the stories and information I was gathering. My professional research and personal experiences with supernatural awareness have confirmed the following truths about supernatural occurrences and those who experience them.

1. Supernatural experiences *can happen anywhere*. People have described experiences happening in their homes, at school, and at work. They've described these experiences occurring while they were traveling in airplanes, cars, or trains or even while they were walking or riding a bike. People have described having supernatural experiences in prisons, hospitals, restaurants, forests, and many other settings and locations.

2. Supernatural experiences *can happen to anyone*, regardless of culture, age, or spiritual beliefs. For example, among the reincarnation cases studied by Dr. Ian Stevenson, a Canadian-born research professor of psychiatry at the University of Virginia, there are numerous cases of young children telling adults things the children could not possibly know, yet the information turned out to be true. I have heard stories of supernatural events from Christians,

Muslims, Buddhists, Wiccans, and those who follow the spiritual beliefs of indigenous peoples, to name a few.

3. Key details of supernatural experiences are often validated by *external information* — in other words, by information or occurrences outside of the experiencer, their immediate environment, and their control. For example, a man told me how, while driving his motorcycle, he had slipped on some sand, lost control of his motorcycle, and was lying on the street, bleeding. He heard a voice in his head say, "If you want to live, get up right now!" He instantly moved, and a moment later, a truck drove over the very spot where he had been lying. Another example: A woman had a vision of her son getting in an accident with an automobile as he rode his bike to the theater, prompting her to call the theater to ask about her son. Later, she learned that the accident was actually occurring at the very same time she was on phone.

4. Some detail about the experience is *connected to events in the experiencer's life or has a particular meaning for them.* For example, one woman told me that every time she met a new person who was going to become a good friend, she smelled her grandmother's perfume, even though there was no logical source for that scent. Another person told me whenever she saw pennies on the ground, she understood they were her mother's way of communicating with her.

5. *Inner and outer aspects of a supernatural experience often fit together in a meaningful way for the experiencer.* For example, in your mind, you might see an object moving in a way that defies the laws of gravity; later, you see the same object in the real world moving exactly the way you first saw it doing so in your mind. Or you might think of someone, and soon after (sometimes immediately after), that person calls you, texts you, or crosses your path.

6. Individuals who've had supernatural experiences *often seek others who have shared similar experiences, in order to validate their experiences.* One individual I interviewed said, "I (my experience) was verified because my friend said other people had seen it (what I'd seen) too." Another person felt validated when a parapsychology class had a séance in her childhood bedroom. Several people in the class reported seeing the image of a man with brown boots and a blue uniform. Their descriptions of him matched those of a man she had seen in that room when she was a child; however, she had not told them about the man or described him to them.

7. Individuals who've had supernatural experiences *often fear being negatively judged by others.* A fifty-nine-year-old Irish married woman reported, "Absolutely nobody in my family believed me. (They said,) 'It is your imagination. You're making it up.' They literally just thought I was making it up to get attention or whatever." A fifty-year-old Italian-American, married man said, "I think that, at the time, I thought my father might think I was fabricating something, and that's why I didn't really tell anybody."

8. Individuals who've had supernatural experiences *are often afraid others will think they're going insane or losing their mind.* Many people I interviewed reported experiencing this particular fear. One person said, "I didn't tell anybody else. I didn't want anyone to think I was nuts." Another told me, "I feel like if I tell people, they will think I am crazy. I don't tell anybody really—only my sister and my best friend. I think it scares them." Yet another person said, "I don't tell anybody about these things anymore because they are going to think I'm crazy."

A thirty-one-year-old, Caucasian, married female, with a bachelor's degree and no religious affiliation, told me, "I think they just thought that I was crazy. They looked at me funny like I was touched in the head or nuts. Some people were receptive to my supernatural experience, but most were not. People just kind of blew me off. They ignored what I wanted to describe. They didn't want to talk about such happenings. They were not... saying I was dreaming but might just as well. 'What kind of medications were you on?' the nurses were saying. 'It is okay just rest' — that kind of thing."

The thirty-one-year-old, married, Catholic retired police officer and mother of three, with a master's degree, was also fearful that others would think there was something wrong with her mind. "I was kind of scared to talk to my husband about it because I think he is going to think I am crazy," she said. "I told him, 'My (dead) ex is following me around.' He laughed it off (saying), 'Is he watching us make out?' ... It makes me nervous to talk in front of other people because I don't want them to think that I'm a whack job or crazy."

9. *It is often difficult for individuals to put their supernatural experiences into words,* because these experiences include details and perceptions that our typical language cannot account for. Words and language tend to shape and limit the descriptive process. One person described her struggle to express her experiences this way: "It seems all very real in my mind. Then when I try and put it into descriptive words, I find that it is so difficult to try and explain that it makes me kind of question myself because I can't put it into any concrete categories. It just raises a lot of questions in my mind. I didn't feel like a quack at the time it happened. I just feel like a quack trying to talk about it, because I don't feel like it's normal." She struggled to find the right words to describe what she had experienced.

10. *During supernatural experiences when individuals are speaking to an entity, that entity often responds accordingly.* For example, when a fifty-nine-year-old married woman, with some college education, saw an image of a man standing next to her bed, she told him to go away, and he did. Another woman asked a ghost to stop turning on the water in the upstairs bathroom, and the faucet never went on again on its own.

11. *The sensory information individuals take in during a supernatural experience is often enhanced, intense, and unusually clear and unclouded.* These sensory details are usually quite vivid and magnified. Colors are brighter than normal. Sounds are especially clear and completely audible. The experiencer's feelings are unusual and not easily replicated.

For example, a thirty-one-year-old, Caucasian, female airport communication dispatcher, of no religious affiliation, reported having the following supernatural experience when she was working as a correctional officer in a federal penitentiary:

So we were coming down from three tier to two tier, which is the first one, and I followed somebody. He was kind of tall. He was about six feet, two or three inches tall, very thin, and slender. He had on the inmate uniform. He also had on a winter hat that they are allowed to have. I'm like, "This is odd. Nobody should be out, and the janitors, they know they have to wait until count and then we open their cells."
So I followed him down the stairs, on the left side of the tier... you have the showers and a few cells, but you also have their satellite gaming area. It used to be a dining facility. They locked a portion of it off, and it is just their gaming area. They still have the steel chairs and other things in there. ...

And there is just one way in and one way out. I go in there. All the doors are locked that lead to other areas, and nobody is in there...

I went in there, and because it used to be a kitchen, I touched all the doors, checked everything, checked all the areas, and nobody went by me. But he wasn't there. That was just weird. I'm thinking to myself, "Okay, where did he go?"

And then I was telling my coworkers, and they were like "Oh, yeah you were just imagining it." No, I saw somebody. I know he was there. I can still clearly see the guy in front of me that I was following...

It's just those things that you never ever forget... I can clearly remember (people), especially when I'm following somebody. I'm short, and so whenever I see, like, you, I'm like, "Wow, he's kind of tall..." This guy was like six feet, two or three inches tall. So for me, I'm like, "Wow, he's pretty tall."

Vivid sensory details often result in exceptionally clear and impactful memories of the event. The former penitentiary guard described the memory of her experience as "burned in my head." Others I interviewed said their experiences were burned in their minds. Years later, they remembered the details of their experiences as clearly as if it happened yesterday.

12. Like other major life events, *supernatural experiences frequently stand out in the minds of those who experience them and frequently result in transformational changes.* They are often life changing or life altering and have an impact on how individuals function. These occurrences are not easily forgotten and often drive experiencers to seek answers and make transformational changes in their lives—changes that are often noted by others. You may remember, for example, the woman in Chapter 4

who, after having an out-of-body experience during an assault, realized the importance of the connections in her world and no longer felt suicidal, as she had before the experience.

Reflections: Think about supernatural experiences you may have had yourself, heard about from others, read about, or seen depicted in a movie, television show, or other video medium. Compare them with the twelve findings described in this chapter. In which of the occurrences can you see each of these findings borne out?

1. Supernatural experiences can happen anywhere.
2. Supernatural experiences can happen to anyone.
3. Key details of supernatural experiences are often validated by external information.
4. Some detail about the experience is connected to events in the experiencer's life or has a particular meaning for them.
5. Inner and outer aspects of a supernatural experience often fit together in a meaningful way for the experiencer.
6. Individuals who've had supernatural experiences often seek others who have shared similar experiences, in order to validate their experiences.
7. Individuals who've had supernatural experiences often fear being negatively judged by others.
8. Individuals who've had supernatural experiences are often afraid others will think they're going crazy.
9. It is often difficult for individuals to put their supernatural experiences into words.
10. When individuals are speaking to an entity, that entity often responds accordingly.

11. The sensory information individuals take in during a supernatural experience is often enhanced, intense, and unusually clear and unclouded.

12. Supernatural experiences frequently stand out in the minds of those who experience them and frequently result in transformational changes.

Chapter 11

Dealing with Skeptics: Diversity of Perceptions

In every important step in the evolution of human beings, there have been stories of divine intervention, guidance, protection, and knowledge of things to come. The authenticity of these experiences was self-evident to those involved in them. There have also been cynics and skeptics who argued and fought to dispute the veracity of such occurrences. If you want to protect and enhance your developing supernatural awareness, it is worth getting to know the skeptics' point of view.

First, remember that maintaining a certain amount of skepticism is healthy when you are developing your supernatural awareness. You must be vigilant to ensure you don't miss simple explanations for events. I had a roommate once say he could hear ghosts knocking in the walls; the source of the noises turned out to be chipmunks. Once while I was helping with a ghost hunt, one of the investigators was trying to talk to the ghosts and said something like, "Can you talk to us or give us a sign?" Then, with a change in voice, she said, really low, "Okay." A co-investigator thought that word was an EVP, and I had to tell him that I'd heard the first individual say it. Another time, we were ghost-hunting in a cemetery and heard the voices of younger women, but we could not see anyone around us. Turns out, there was a path to a lake not far away, and voices easily carried across the water. We must be careful to not see things we want to when they are really not there.

It is also important to remember that some phenomena may seem supernatural now only because we humans have not yet discovered or do not fully understand the natural explanations for them. People could deny that bacteria existed until the microscope was discovered and they could see those unicellular microorganisms for themselves. Such unveiling of what is actual is true of all discoveries to come. So if a supernatural experience does have a logical, real-world explanation, an explanation may eventually appear as our human knowledge of the world grows.

Not all skeptics are wrong all the time. But people's skepticism can be upsetting and challenging when you have had a meaningful and, you believe, authentic interaction with the supernatural. When skeptics become bothersome, understanding the following about them may be useful. These points come from my interactions with skeptics during my research.

1. Skeptics have no experience that allows them to understand something so different from their point of view. They have no inner reference point to compare supernatural experiences to. They may have beliefs or fears that interfere with their ability to perceive something so different. Or they may have training that would become obsolete or invalid if an experience was proven to be a true interaction with the supernatural.

2. Skeptics project their point of view onto whatever is examined. They rationalize any thoughts or experiences of others that are different from theirs, denying anything new is possible. Where some people can learn from mistakes in their perceiving awareness and become more flexible, skeptics allow healthy skepticism to turn into unhealthy closed-mindedness. Most of the individuals whose cases were included in this book were exposed to an experience so different from their everyday reality that it altered their world in a way they hadn't imagined or anticipated. Therefore, they developed a broader view of what's possible in the universe. However, the skeptic doesn't think other possibilities are available.

3. A skeptic is someone whose mind is not yet open enough to have a supernatural experience. Otherwise, there is no zone, territory, or hierarchy of power that a person must get to in order to have supernatural awareness. Anyone can have supernatural awareness pretty much any time, in just about any circumstance.

4. Supernatural experiences often cannot be physically explained or verified as they are typically very personal events unwitnessed by others. Can I prove in an empirical manner that I heard a disembodied voice tell me to check the land deeds for my ancestors as I was doing genealogical research in my state library? No, I cannot. But this does not mean that such an event could not have happened. If the inner voice tells you something that is meaningful to you, no one else can prove or disprove such an experience did or did not happen. But skeptics will instantly reject such information as irrelevant and not worthy of investigation—unless, of course, they are going to try to disprove it.

Reflections: Remember, perception is all the ways we take in information about our universe. Diverse perceptions demonstrate that there are many accurate and flexible ways of seeing something. Our perception is limited only by our past experiences and prior learning.

Exercises: Any of the following three options can help you practice broadening your perspective to include new possibilities.

1. When you have a new or unusual situation, think about the many possible different ways you can perceive or understand it. How many possibilities can you come up with?

2. Try uniquely new things. One mother told me how she and her daughter used to buy a new food every week when they went grocery shopping. Sometimes they found foods that they never knew they would really like. Other times they didn't really like the new food. Either way, they expanded their awareness and knowledge of different foods. How can you use this experiment or a variation of it in your life?

3. How many things can you imagine that are real in the universe, but you have never experienced personally?

Endnotes

Chapter 1: Making a Connection

1. Fredrick Woodard, "A Phenomenological Study of Spontaneous Spiritual and Paranormal Experiences in a 21st Century Sample of Normal People," *Psychological Reports* 110 (2012): 73-132. Fredrick J. Woodard, "A Phenomenological and Perceptual Research Methodology for Understanding Hypnotic Experiencing," *Psychological Reports* 95 (2004): 887-904.

Chapter 3: The First Thought That Comes into Your Mind

2. Fredrick Woodard, "A Phenomenological Study of Spontaneous Spiritual and Paranormal Experiences in a 21st Century Sample of Normal People," *Psychological Reports* 110 (2012): 73-132.

3. J.W. Dunne, *An Experiment with Time* (Charlottesville, VA: Hampton Roads, 2001).

Chapter 4: Altering Time and Space

4. Stanley Krippner, "An Experiment in Dream Telepathy with 'The Grateful Dead,'" *Journal of the American Society of Psychosomatic Dentistry and Medicine* 20 (1973): 9-17.

5. Carl Sextus, *Hypnotism: A Correct Guide to the Science and How Subjects Are Influenced* (Hollywood, CA: Wilshire Book Company, 1957).

6. C. Bernard Ruffin, *Padre Pio: The True Story* (Huntington, IN: Our Sunday Visitor, 1991).

Chapter 7: Perceiving Unexpected Beings and Objects

7. Martin Caidin, *Ghosts of the Air: True Stories of Aerial Hauntings* (New York, NY: Bantam Books, 1991), 268-283.

8. Fredrick Woodard, *Perceptual Hypnosis: A Spiritual Journey Toward Expanding Awareness* (Atglen, PA: REDFeather, 2018), 153-159.

Chapter 9: Ethical Supernatural Awareness: Using Your Gifts Responsibly

9. William J. Baldwin, *Healing Lost Souls: Releasing Unwanted Spirits from Your Energy Body* (Charlottesville, VA: Hampton Roads Publishing, 2003).

10. Shakuntala Modi, *Remarkable Healings: A Psychiatrist Discovers Unsuspected Roots of Mental and Physical Illness* (Charlottesville, VA: Hampton Roads Publishing, 1997).

11. Fredrick Woodard, *Perceptual Hypnosis: A Spiritual Journey Toward Expanding Awareness* (Atglen, PA: REDFeather, 2018), 153-159.

6TH
BOOKS

ALL THINGS PARANORMAL

Investigations, explanations and deliberations on the paranormal, supernatural, explainable or unexplainable. 6th Books seeks to give answers while nourishing the soul: whether making use of the scientific model or anecdotal and fun, but always beautifully written.

Titles cover everything within parapsychology: how to, lifestyles, alternative medicine, beliefs, myths and theories.

If you have enjoyed this book, why not tell other readers by posting a review on your preferred book site?

Recent bestsellers from 6th Books are:

The Scars of Eden
Paul Wallis
How do we distinguish between our ancestors' ideas of God
and close encounters of an extraterrestrial kind?
Paperback: 978-1-78904-852-0 ebook: 978-1-78904-853-7

The Afterlife Unveiled
What the dead are telling us about their world!
Stafford Betty
What happens after we die? Spirits speaking through mediums
know, and they want us to know. This book unveils their
world...
Paperback: 978-1-84694-496-3 ebook: 978-1-84694-926-5

Harvest: The True Story of Alien Abduction
G L Davies
G. L. Davies's most-terrifying investigation yet reveals one
woman's terrifying ordeal of alien visitation, nightmarish
visions and a prophecy of destruction on a scale never before
seen in Pembrokeshire's peaceful history.
Paperback: 978-1-78904-385-3 ebook: 978-1-78904-386-0

Wisdom from the Spirit World
Carole J. Obley
What can those in spirit teach us about the enduring bond of
love, the immense power of forgiveness, discovering our life's
purpose and finding peace in a frantic world?
Paperback: 978-1-78904-302-0 ebook: 978-1-78904-303-7

Spirit Release
Sue Allen
A guide to psychic attack, curses, witchcraft, spirit
attachment, possession, soul retrieval, haunting, deliverance,
exorcism and more, as taught at the College of Psychic
Studies.
Paperback: 978-1-84694-033-0 ebook: 978-1-84694-651-6

Advanced Psychic Development
Becky Walsh
Learn how to practise as a professional, contemporary
spiritual medium.
Paperback: 978-1-84694-062-0 ebook: 978-1-78099-941-8

Where After
Mariel Forde Clarke
A journey that will compel readers to view life after death
in a completely different way.
Paperback: 978-1-78904-617-5 ebook: 978-1-78904-618-2

Poltergeist! A New Investigation into
Destructive Haunting
John Fraser
Is the Poltergeist "syndrome" the only type of paranormal
phenomena that can really be proven?
Paperback: 978-1-78904-397-6 ebook: 978-1-78904-398-3

A Little Bigfoot: On the Hunt in Sumatra
Pat Spain
Pat Spain lost a layer of skin, pulled leeches off his nether
regions, and was violated by an Orangutan for this book
Paperback: 978-1-78904-605-2 ebook: 978-1-78904-606-9

Astral Projection Made Easy
and overcoming the fear of death
Stephanie June Sorrell
From the popular Made Easy series, Astral Projection
Made Easy helps to eliminate the fear of death through
discussion of life beyond the physical body.
Paperback: 978-1-84694-611-0 ebook: 978-1-78099-225-9

Haunted: Horror of Haverfordwest
G.L. Davies
Blissful beginnings for a young couple turn into a nightmare
after purchasing their dream home in Wales in 1989.
Paperback: 978-1-78535-843-2 ebook: 978-1-78535-844-9

Readers of ebooks can buy or view any of these bestsellers by clicking on the live link in the title. Most titles are published in paperback and as an ebook. Paperbacks are available in traditional bookshops. Both print and ebook formats are available online.

Find more titles and sign up to our readers' newsletter at
www.6th-books.com

Join the 6th books Facebook group at
6th Books The world of the Paranormal